Wine, Women, & Death

Wine, Women, & Death

Medieval Hebrew Poems on the Good Life

Raymond P. Scheindlin

THE JEWISH PUBLICATION SOCIETY
Philadelphia·New York·Jerusalem   5747·1986

Copyright © 1986 by The Jewish Publication Society
First edition   All rights reserved
Manufactured in the United States of America

Library of Congress Cataloging in Publication Data
Wine, women, and death.
  English and Hebrew.
  Bibliography: p. 179
  Includes index.
  1. Hebrew poetry, Medieval—Translations into English.
2. Hebrew poetry, Medieval.   3. English poetry—Translations from He-
brew.   I. Scheindlin, Raymond P.
PJ5059.E3W56   1986   892.4'12'08   86–2958
ISBN 0–8276–0266–9

Parts of Chapters 1 and 2 appeared originally in the journal Prooftexts *and*
are reprinted here with the permission of The Johns Hopkins University Press.

Designed by Adrianne Onderdonk Dudden

The illustrations in the text, rendered by Linda R. Turner, are based on medi-
eval motifs found in Henry George Farmer, Islam, *Leipzig, Deutscher Verlag*
für Musik, 1966.

To Janice with love

Contents

Foreword

Jewish writers like to stress what is unique about Judaism. This book deals with what Judaism had in common with the world around it during a particular period, the Hebrew Golden Age in tenth- to twelfth-century Spain. My intention is not apologetic, like that of the nineteenth-century historians who labored to convince themselves and others that Jews are part of humanity at large. That battle has been won. I wish to present the Jewish poets of medieval Spain as a reminder that Jews can assimilate the values and styles of the outside world without betraying their historic responsibility to their people, and by doing so may even contribute to the future genuinely Jewish achievements of enduring worth.

The book was conceived on a cold midnight in December several years ago, when I returned to Brooklyn Heights after delivering a lecture on the Hebrew poetry of the Golden Age at a synagogue in remotest Westchester. I had the good luck to encounter my good friend, songwriter Annie Dinerman, who was delighted with the title of my lecture—Wine, Women, and Death. It was her imagination that, in the space of an hour's conversation, turned the lecture into a book. Annie's enthusiasm for this project has never waned; neither has my desire to thank her in public, as I am now doing.

I have also been looking forward to acknowledging the help of Professor Stephen A. Geller, who worked through many of the translations with me. With his exquisite sense of rhythm and diction, refined by years of studying poetry in many languages, he helped me think through my work and to sharpen it.

My thanks are also offered to Hugo Weisgall for nagging me to finish this book whenever he saw my attention wandering; to Professor Seymour Feldman for advising me on some philosophical matters; to Professors Ivan Marcus and Menahem Schmelzer for their helpful comments; to the Dr. Nisson Touroff Fund of the Jewish Theological Seminary for a summer research grant; to my son Dov for doing part of the typing and many of the clerical chores; and to my daughter Dahlia for helping me with the proofreading. I dedicate this book to Janice Meyerson as a small token that comes nowhere near expressing the fullness of my gratitude.

Wine, Women, & Death

Introduction

"In the days of Ḥasdai the Nasi they began to chirp, and in the days of Samuel the Nagid they sang aloud."[1] To a medieval chronicler reflecting on the beginnings of Hebrew culture in Muslim Spain, no image could have seemed more appropriate to the spirit of the age than bird song. Although poetry had been a major outlet for Jewish religious feeling since late antiquity, in the time of Ḥasdai Ibn Shaprut the Nasi (c. 915–970) it gained renewed prestige, acquiring new social functions and themes to become the period's characteristic literary form. In retrospect, the age seemed to be a kind of cultural dawn, a fresh beginning in the history of Judaism, its poets the songbirds that accompanied its rise. What is most satisfying about this image is that its chirping birds allude to a whole set of associations that figure prominently in the imaginative life of medieval Andalusians: Jews, Arabs, and Mozarabs alike.

The medieval Andalusian's favorite pastime, his dearest fantasy, and one of his most beloved literary themes was the enjoyment of nature in spring. The scene might be a river bank, a grassy hillside, a palace garden or simply the patio of a small dwelling, such as may

3

still be seen everywhere in southern Spain; but always there is fresh grass, a gentle breeze, running water, and the chirping of birds. The Andalusian obsession with such gentle outdoor delights is reflected even in book titles. It may not be remarkable that an anthology of Arabic poems about gardens in spring should be called *The Extraordinary: On the Description of Spring* or even that a book of love poetry should be called *The Book of Gardens;* but when we find a geography entitled *The Perfumed Garden: On the History of Districts,* or a biography entitled *The Flowers of the Garden: The Life of Qadi ʿIyyad,* or another entitled *The Fragrant Breeze from the Verdant Bough of Andalusia: On the Life of its Vizier Lisan al-Din Ibn al-Khatib,* we are convinced that the garden in spring was a cultural symbol of primary significance.

In tenth-century Spain there was a circle of wealthy Jews, thoroughly educated in Arabic language and literature, skilled in professions, and holding positions of responsibility and power in public life, who were also pious, learned, and fiercely loyal to Jewish interests. These extraordinary men, sometimes known as the Andalusian courtier rabbis, were not the first medieval Jews to take part in the life of the larger world, for Jews in tenth-century Iraq had functioned in the courts of the Abbasid caliphs. What was unique about the Andalusian Jewish courtiers was the self-conscious way in which they synthesized the dominant Arabic-Islamic culture with Jewish religious and literary traditions. These men, who founded a new type of Jewish life, based on a novel educational program and geared to producing a new leadership, sought literary expression in a completely renovated poetry. For these Jews, religious commitment, cultural identification, and national loyalty were strong enough and flexible enough to permit them to enter openly into the life and style of the dominant culture while remaining Jews. The Andalusian Muslim ruling class of the time was sufficiently worldly and tolerant in its religious outlook to welcome them as participants; the price was acculturation, but not conversion. To the Jews who benefited from the opportunity to join the brilliant material and intellectual life of Andalusian-Moorish culture, which in the tenth century was at its peak, the world must have seemed one great wine party held in the enormous lush garden of Spain—and they themselves a uniquely gifted generation.[2]

In the world of the Muslim ruling class, literature, particularly poetry, enjoyed enormous prestige. Linguistic studies—grammar, lexicography, and rhetoric—were the basis of education. The intellectual formation of the Muslim aristocracy was based on intense application to a corpus of classical literary texts in a language which, though similar to the dialect in daily use, was distinct from it and required systematic study. These texts provided a classic cultural model distinct from the religious tradition, rooted in and deriving its values from the world of the pre-Islamic Bedouin tribesmen. This model was somewhat in conflict with the monotheistic religious values of the Quran and Hadith; it provided a secular valence to a life in which religious values and observances played a very great part.

Jews learned the Arabic language and literary models not by passively absorbing them from the environment but through concentrated study; their aim was to be part of the highest level of a society that judged a man largely by his social graces, linguistic skills, and literary taste. Pious and loyal Jews enjoined their sons to apply themselves with all assiduousness to the study of the Arabic grammarians and rhetoricians. The Jewish boys who labored at conning the pre-Islamic tribal poetry were at no great disadvantage vis-à-vis their Muslim friends, for both spoke the same dialectical Arabic and, as the children of wealthy city folk, were equally distant culturally from the exotic yet dreary life portrayed by the ancient poets. Since the values inculcated by the study of these poets were outside the Islamic religious system, Jewish boys had no religious inhibitions against studying, absorbing, and eventually even loving them.

So thoroughly did the Jewish upper class assimilate the Arabic literary tradition that they eventually synthesized it with their Jewish literary heritage, creating almost overnight a new Hebrew literature that derived many of its concerns, principles, images, and even rhythms from Arabic. Protégés of the Jewish physician Hasdai Ibn Shaprut, a courtier in the service of the Spanish caliph ʿAbd al-Raḥman III (912–961), devised ways to adapt Hebrew verse to the rhythmic patterns of Arabic, developed a formal rhetorical style for official correspondence, compiled Hebrew dictionaries, pioneered the study of Hebrew grammar, and bestowed on the Bible, in addition to its traditional role as the source of religious authority, the new role of literary classic. They also began writing secular poetry.

In the Arab courts, the language of poetry was exclusively Arabic. Among themselves, the Jewish courtiers, who were the leaders and authorities of the Jewish community, also spoke Arabic; but from the time of Ibn Shaprut, they began to compose poetry in Hebrew to perform in their circle the same functions as Arabic poetry performed outside.

Much of the Arabic and Hebrew poetry of medieval Andalusia was courtly panegyric: eulogies of friends, patrons, or allies intended partly to flatter the recipient, partly to shape public opinion in a world in which poetry was the chief form of publicity. Related to panegyric in function were satirical poems, in which the enemies of the poet or his patron were lampooned, and funeral laments, really a species of panegyric. These three genres are united by their predominantly political function as instruments for the regulation of interpersonal relations within the ruling class. As such they are serious works of substantial length, thematic complexity, and a studied, formal character.

But poetry was also composed for simple amusement. Members of the courtier class, Muslims and Jews, entertained each other by listening to poetry, reciting their own verses, discussing those of others, and setting themes for improvisation for one another. In the introduction to Chapter I we shall look more closely into the social context of such light verse. These poems are short, stylized treatments of certain conventional themes. They deal, for the most part, with the pleasures of life enjoyed by the Andalusian courtiers, and the regret that life is so short and pleasures so transient. It is this kind of poetry that is the subject of this book.

The conventions, imagery, and cultural background of the new Hebrew poetry are clearly identifiable as belonging to the Arabic literary milieu that spawned it, but there is also a sense in which this poetry is part of the mainstream of Western culture. For the first time since the Bible, Hebrew writing in the Golden Age dealt not only with religion and the covenant between God and the Jews, but also with categories of experience common to all mankind, and in terms more or less common to Greek and Roman literature and the secular Latin poetry of medieval Christendom.

Though these Jews speak with a Middle Eastern accent, their language is universal, their subject matter shared by the *Greek Anthology,* the *Carmina Burana,* and, for that matter, Gustav Mahler's *Das Lied von der Erde.*

Not that they were simply secularists. The very poets who sang of the pleasures of life in their secular verse also composed poetry for the synagogue as convincing as that of the liturgical poets of Byzantine Palestine or the eleventh-century Rhineland, whose piety was far less adulterated. The courtier-rabbis inhabited two worlds, and as long as their political and social status was stable, they did not dwell on the contradictions between them. Here and there we find, even in this anthology, evidence of uneasiness about the synthesis. But for the most part, they sang in the synagogue of God and Israel, and in their gardens, of human pleasures and worldly wisdom.

The gardens of medieval Hebrew poetry provide it with a setting in nature, but it is not a very "natural" nature.[3] Often the gardens were actually patios, like the Lions' Court of the Alhambra, enclosed by a building to form a completely artificial environment. There might be a fountain in the center, feeding a pool or little canals that irrigated carefully designed flower beds. Beside the pool or along the canals might be deer or lions carved in stone; around the garden a colonnade, the columns representing stylized palm trees with birds in their boughs and carved arabesque foliage. In such a garden, nature has been utterly subdued by art. Sitting there, one might lose the sense of boundary between the artificial and the real. The picture, and the fantasy it inspires, was gloriously painted by Ibn Gabirol:

> . . . .
> A full pool, like Solomon's basin,
>   But not standing upon cattle,
> Lions positioned on its edge,
>   Like whelps crying for prey,
> Whose insides, like fountains, pour
>   Streams like rivers through their mouths.
> And deer planted by the canals,
>   Hollow, for water to spill out,
> To sprinkle the flowers in the beds,
>   And to pour clear water on the sod,

. . . .
And birds singing aloud in the boughs,
    Peering from atop the palm-fronds,
And fresh anemone blossoms,
    Roses, nard, and camphor,
All competing with each other,
    Though they are all choice in our sight.
The camphor blossoms say, "We are (so)
    White, we rule over the stars."
The doves coo, in their own way,
    And say, "We are lords over the turtledoves."
. . . .
The deer rise up against the girls (?)
    And cover their beauty with beauties, (?)
Boasting together against them,
    For they are like young bucks.
And when the sun rises over them
    I say to it, "Be still! Do not exceed the bounds!"
. . . . [4]

In this passage the boundary between inanimate objects and living beings is deliciously vague. After hearing about the stone lions and deer, and the passing reference to the bronze cattle of Solomon's basin, we might be justified in assuming that the birds and palm fronds are also stone. Yet at least, some of the flowers may be real, for they are being watered. Whether stone or real, all the objects in the garden become animated and personified in the fantastic boasting match toward the end of the passage, where unfortunately the Hebrew becomes somewhat obscure. But the meaning of the last verse is perfectly clear. Quoting Joshua, the poet tells the sun to halt in its course; the same sweeping command silences the angry animation of the preceding lines, suddenly restoring the now cacophonous garden to its former paradisiac tranquillity, and turning the animals back to stone—a kind of reverse miracle.[5] The whole passage is a triumph of artifice.

Even when the scene is truly outdoors, it is a tame hillside or a river bank on which the poet reclines in tranquil contemplation of nature's beauty, never a dark forest, crashing waterfall, frightful cliff, or a destructive, raging storm. The rare depictions of the brutal, chaotic, mysterious faces of nature occur only in highly personal poetry, not in conventional genres.

The courtiers' preference for nature in a controlled state is paralleled by their preference in poetic form. As opposed to ordinary speech, called in Arabic *nathr,* "scattered words," poetry is called *naẓm,* "arranged words," the very terminology implying a hierarchy based on formal organization. Rhymed prose, used in the oracles of pre-Islamic soothsayers, in the Quran, and, later, in the formal epistles of courtly correspondence and certain types of narrative, is superior to ordinary prose in this hierarchy. In its earlier form, as found in the Quran, rhymed prose consisted of strings of short rhyming phrases or clauses; there was no particular regularity in the number of phrases in each rhyming group. But in the rhymed prose of medieval courtly writing there is a strong tendency for the rhyming phrases to come in rhythmically balanced pairs. This rhythmic balancing reaches the highest degree of organization in poetry. In formal Arabic verse every line is composed of two metrically identical parts; the first half of each verse sets up a powerful demand in the mind of the auditor for a complementary second half. The two halves are not rhymed (except optionally in the first verse of a poem), for the rhyme is used to link the ends of the verses. But whatever the poem's meter, the rise and fall of its two verse-halves always constitute its basic rhythm.[6]

This habit of rhythmic balancing has an analogue in the rhetorical style used throughout the history of Arabic poetry and particularly favored in medieval Andalusia.[7] The poetry abounds in word plays that characteristically involve a correspondence between a word and its opposite, a word and its homophone, or a word used at the beginning of the verse and repeated at the verse's end. Imagery too deals in correspondences. A poem describing a beautiful girl is more likely to be built out of a list of her features, each one compared with a different flower, than out of an extended metaphor in which her whole self is assimilated into another order of being. Particularly beloved is the juxtaposition of opposite characteristics: A beautiful girl has the eyes of a doe and the heart of a lion; a patron's hand is hard as rock (against his enemies) but wet as the ocean (in pouring benefactions upon his protégés); a wine cup gleams like fire but feels like ice; and so forth. The object in which the two opposite characteristics resides thus becomes a site of balance and harmony, wherein conflicting tendencies are resolved.

8250

The quest for balance and harmony is particularly important in the garden poetry:

> Winter wrote with the ink of its rains and showers,
> The pen of its flashing lightning, and the hand of its clouds
> A letter upon the garden in blue and purple,
> Of which no craftsman with all his skill could make the like,
> Therefore, when the earth longed to see the sky,
> She embroidered on the twigs of her flowerbeds something like the stars.[8]

Although the many rhetorical and rhythmical devices used to make the point are not evident in the translation, the basic movement of the poem does not depend on the original language. The sky writes a letter to the ground in the form of flowers, and the earth responds with a gift in the form of stars. On the level of the imagery, the reciprocity is perfect. But this ideal rhetorical reciprocity is only a trick of the poet's imagination, for although the flowers are real, the stars are not. The sky *can* make flowers; the ground can make only *imitation* stars. In the flowers, both longings are fulfilled, and this union is effected entirely by means of rhetoric.

Medieval Arabic and Hebrew courtly poetry attempt to capture the aristocratic ideals of harmony, balance, and control in the medium of rhythm and rhetoric. The poem's role with respect to feelings is similar to that of the formal garden's stone animals and palm trees with respect to nature. Thus the poem is itself a kind of garden. As the Arab poet al-Muʿtamid Ibn ʿAbbad says of one of his *qaṣidas:*

> Here is a garden of thought whose bed is watered
> By the bounty of your hand, not by dew or rain.
> I have made your name the flowers within it;
> At all times there is fruit for him who wishes to pick it.[9]

On the Hebrew side, Moses Ibn Ezra says of his own poetry: Come into the garden of my verse and find balm / For your sorrow; there rejoice like one who sings.[10]

Since poetry makes use of gardens as a typical theme and a source of imagery, and since it is conceived to be a kind of garden, it is not surprising that certain kinds of verse, especially that presented in this anthology, were typically recited in gardens. We shall describe the entertainments of the medieval courtiers in more detail in the introduction to Chapter I. For now let us simply note that when a wine party was held in a garden and a poet recited verse describing a wine party in a garden, the poem functioned both as an instrument of the evening's entertainment and as an idealized concretization of it, just as the garden is a concretization of nature. Such poems form a magic circle with their own social setting.

It might seem from what has been said so far that the poetry of the medieval Andalusian courtiers was entirely stereotyped in content and technique. This inference requires some modification, for poets in both languages learned to manipulate the conventional resources of the poetic tradition to give voice to their own personal visions and to display their own inner worlds. Much of the work of the four great Hebrew poets of the Golden Age reveals the highly individualistic personalities of extremely sensitive men. Their individuality cannot, however, be seen clearly except against the background of the tremendous body of conventional materials that they held in common with each other and with the other poets of their time and place and is revealed through their manipulation of the conventions rather than direct statements. This anthology deals exclusively with the themes in which the conventional predominates, because its purpose is to display the character not of the poets as individuals but of their class as a whole. Even so, these four poets are too great to be muzzled by an anthologist's selectivity, and I have gladly called attention to their personal traits when they appear. It will be useful for the reader's orientation to introduce them.

Samuel the Nagid (993–1055 or 1056) rose from obscurity to become vizier of the ruler of Granada, which like most of the great cities of Muslim Spain was an independent state through most of the eleventh century. He was thus the most powerful Jew of the Middle Ages. In addition to his responsibilities at court, he found time to manage the affairs of the Jewish community and to engage in a wide range of literary activities. Author of a Hebrew grammar, treatises on the Talmud, and three volumes of secular poetry, he is the very archetype of the courtier-rabbi.

Solomon Ibn Gabirol (c. 1020–c. 1057) lived in relative obscurity, though he seems for a time to have been in the circle of Samuel the Nagid and to have received the patronage of a distinguished courtier of Saragossa, Yequtiel Ibn Ḥassan. Physically weak, a social misfit, he devoted his life to philosophy, composing a treatise on ethics and another on metaphysics. This completely secular magnum opus, the *Source of Life,* belongs to the common field of medieval philosophy rather than to Jewish theology: Ibn Gabirol's intellectual career, like the political career of the Nagid, was in the larger world. Besides his secular poetry he also composed a great quantity of liturgical poetry.

Moses Ibn Ezra (c. 1055–after 1135) belonged to a family prominent in the court of Granada and its Jewish community. Raised to wealth, power, and high culture, he found his world shattered by the fall of the city-states of Andalusia to the Almoravide Berbers in 1090, when his family fled the city. After leaving Granada himself, he spent the second half of his life in various cities of northern Spain, lamenting his isolation and the loss of his cultural circle. He composed several treatises on literary theory, two of which are extant, and a large quantity of secular and liturgical poetry.[11]

Judah Halevi (before 1075–1141) brings the Golden Age to a close chronologically. Only a few years after his death, a new Berber dynasty, the Almohades, occupied Andalusia and instituted religious persecutions that resulted in the abandonment of southern Spain by its Jewish leadership. Curiously, Halevi's life also reflects a turning away from the ideals of the courtier-rabbi class. At about age fifty, after a lifetime as a *bon vivant,* literary figure, physician, and Jewish communal leader, he decided to withdraw from the world and to devote himself to religion. Setting out by ship for Palestine, he disembarked in Alexandria, where the cultural and social life threatened to draw him back into a world similar to the one he had so daringly abandoned. He finally reached the Holy Land, and shortly thereafter died, leaving behind him a theological treatise and quantities of secular and religious poetry.

These four poets are distinguished partly by the sheer volume of the poetry they left behind. Many other poets are known by name but represented by fewer poems. Medieval notices indicate that some of these seemingly minor poets must have also been prolific and gifted; but it is hard to measure them against the four great poets because of the paucity of the works definitely assigned to them. The vast quantities of anonymous poems extant from the Golden Age include many fine individual pieces that on the whole tell more about the period than the poets. This anthology contains a few poems by minor poets, each an important literary figure of his time.

Dunash ben Labrat (mid−tenth century), a scholar and grammarian, was a protégé of Ḥasdai Ibn Shaprut, the first important Jewish courtier in Muslim Spain. Before coming to Spain he had been a disciple of the great rabbinic authority of tenth-century Iraq, Saadia Gaon, and had devised a way to adapt the prosodic conventions of Arabic to Hebrew. This breakthrough provided Jewish literati with an important tool for developing the new Hebrew poetry treated in this book.

Isaac Ibn Khalfon (mid-tenth century−c. 1020) is said to have been the first Hebrew poet to make his living from poetry. Little of literary importance is known of his life except that, like Ibn Gabirol, he enjoyed the patronage of Samuel the Nagid and of Yequtiel Ibn Ḥassan of Saragossa.

Abraham Ibn Ezra (1089−1164), friend of Judah Halevi, left Spain in the wake of the Almohade invasion to wander throughout western Europe and the Middle East, disseminating Golden Age culture by composing treatises on a variety of learned topics. Though his treatises mostly deal with astronomy, mathematics, and grammar, his fame derives from his Bible commentaries, which unite a typically rationalistic approach to the text through grammar and lexicography with an essentially neo-Platonic view of the world. A daunting mass of liturgical and some secular poetry is attributed to Ibn Ezra.

These are the poets whose work has been selected for the anthology. Perhaps it is unfair to them as artists, but I have made the selection without any regard to the individual character their work reveals. The Hebrew poetry of the Golden Age is hardly known at all outside learned circles, but what is available in English is almost always presented in a biographical framework. My purpose here is to expose the culture as a whole through its most typical form of expression. I believe that it is important to do so because the Hebrew culture of the Golden Age shows an aspect of Judaism once highly developed but now losing respectability; that is, the ability to absorb the values and the style of the outside world and to re-shape itself accordingly, without losing the sense of Jewish identity. Samuel the Nagid and Moses Ibn Ezra did not need to cultivate nostalgia for an idyllic past in order to feel like Jews. They were worldly men, and the Judaism they lived was cosmopolitan in nature, unafraid of the challenges of contemporary morality, philosophy, and literary modes. The contrast between their culture and that of other medieval—and some modern—Jewish communities is powerfully conveyed in the secular Hebrew poetry they composed. It is my hope that wider acquaintance with the unique character of their world may contribute to a reappraisal of the nature of Jewish life.

In the hope that the poems will be read not only for their documentary value but also for their original purpose, entertainment, I have tried to reconstruct the literary experience that the medieval poets were aiming to achieve. The Hebrew text is provided partly so that the reader familiar with the Hebrew alphabet can read the poems metrically. The translations are in verse and attempt a tone roughly equivalent to that of the Hebrew.

Every translation calls for a statement of purpose. Faced with the impossibility of capturing each aspect of the original in another language, the translator is forced to perform triage on his text, selecting some aspects to reproduce, abandoning others. He owes the reader an explanation of the principles that underlie his choices.

The decision to translate into verse necessitates sacrificing the lexical precision that is possible in prose. I have given rhythm priority over philological accuracy because the culture was one in which style mattered greatly. A woodenly accurate prose translation distorts more than a loose but lilting translation. I deviate from the meaning of the original only as far as my sense of responsibility to the Hebrew language and its Golden Age allows. The reader is free to follow my reasoning, since all other English translations known to me are cited in the notes. In the notes I also cite a source, in most cases the anthology of Ḥayyim Schirmann, through which the scholarly reader can track down most of the other editions and apparatus that he needs to criticize my renditions. In the most important cases I have saved him the trouble, by remarking in the discussion on liberties taken.

Like the original poets, who had no compunctions whatsoever about this preference, I have favored rhythm and rhetoric over natural diction and word order. My main intent is not to write graceful English poems, but to try to find English rhythmical, rhetorical, and lexical equivalents for the original Hebrew poems. Archaisms and inversions are part of the experience. In citing the Bible I have generally followed the new Jewish Publication Society translation, though I have occasionally used the Jewish Publication Society's version of 1917 or my own rendering.

Before describing the verse forms of the translations, I must describe those of the Hebrew originals. The Golden Age poets, beginning with Dunash ben Labrat, grafted onto the Hebrew language a metrical principle foreign to it—the quantitative principle known to them from Arabic verse, but common also to Greek and classical Latin. This meter is based on the alternation of long and short vowel quantities, rather than that of stressed and unstressed syllables as in English. The natural stress sometimes agrees with the meter, but more often conflicts with it. For the purposes of Hebrew, all vowels are considered long except those reduced to schwa and the conjunction *u*. Long and short vowels occur according to certain canonical patterns. This is not the place to explain the system in detail; the first line of each Hebrew poem is scanned so that the reader can read metrically even without fully understanding the system.[12]

Golden Age secular poems all belong to one of two prosodic types. The majority use a single metrical pattern and rhyme throughout. This basic form of Arabic poetry derives from the *qaṣidas* of the pre-Islamic Bedouin tribes, and until the last century was considered the only form suited to serious Arabic poetry. In these poems, every verse has two metrically identical halves, or hemistichs, which by their continual rise and fall lend the verse its distinctive rhythm. The Andalusian Arabs of the tenth century introduced a new type of verse in strophes, known as *muwashshah*. These poems were intended for a more musical type of performance than the *qaṣida*-type poems, which were recited in a sing-song. *Muwashshaḥāt* were sung to instrumental accompaniment, their first verse probably serving as a refrain. Though the poet had great freedom in constructing the strophes, the general pattern was always the same: Each strophe consists of two groups of lines, the first group with a rhyme that changes from strophe to strophe, and the second with a rhyme that remains constant throughout the poem. Often the two groups differ in meter. The final constant rhyme group, known as the *kharja*, ends the poem. It is either in vernacular Arabic or in the Mozarabic hybrid of Romance and Arabic, though Hebrew *muwashshaḥāt* often end simply in Hebrew.[13]

In choosing the verse patterns of the translations, my first consideration has been to imitate the literary level of the original. Since the primary effect of using Arabic quantitative meter in Hebrew was to establish the poem, whatever its contents, as serious literature, ordinary blank verse seemed the most appropriate English meter to suggest most of the conventional meters of the monorhymed poems. I did not attempt to use English monorhyme except in one or two epigrams, because English does not possess the rhyming capability of a Semitic language. The iambic pentameter cadence is sufficiently familiar to the ears of English speakers to provide the rise and fall of the two hemistichs without the confirmation of the rhyme. Where the poet used word plays or other devices to get significant rhythmic effects I felt free to alter the meter or use any other device that would suggest the character of the original. In cases in which the Hebrew meter was very distinctive, I used other English meters. In the strophic poems I was usually unable to find a rhyme to link all the strophes, and so I regretfully abandoned this important feature of the originals.

The discussions of the poems are intended not as complete commentaries but as guides to their appreciation and an understanding of their cultural significance. Their rhetorical effects and biblical allusions are noted and explained when necessary for the interpretation of the poem as a whole or relevant to the point under discussion: Pointing out every one would be tedious for the non-specialist. In the discussions I try to show what feature of the Hebrew is imitated by some peculiarity in the translation, and why it was chosen; and occasionally the discussion points out a feature of the original that I was not able to capture. In rare instances when the translation is based on an emended or unintelligible Hebrew text, the fact is noted in either the discussion or the notes. It was sometimes hard to refrain from detailed treatment of technical problems, but this book is not meant for specialists. If I dwell occasionally on matters of grammar and syntax, it is because this book is meant for readers who care about language.

As for the selection of the poems, I have chosen only whole poems and mostly short ones, on subjects that can be understood without complicated explanations of Islamic or Jewish arcana. They are classified under the three headings Wine, Women, and Death, and within the sections they are arranged in an order that allows me to present the material in a natural sequence. I have tried to choose poems that are interesting in their own right, but which also illustrate those themes of Golden Age culture that are the subject of this book.

1
Wine

Hebrew poetry about wine presupposes a communal situation in which wine is drunk, so in order to appreciate the poetry it is useful to have some knowledge of the social institution from which it derived: the wine party. Although copious prose sources describe the wine drinking practices of the Andalusian Muslims, we have next to no documentation, other than the poetry itself, for this aspect of Jewish life. Since the Hebrew and Arabic poetry are so similar in content, it seems reasonable to begin by describing some of the practices of the dominant group, and to assume that they apply to Jews as well.

The Andalusian practice was to introduce the wine after dinner. As they did in antiquity, the drinkers sat on cushions placed around the room, with little tables by their side. The wine was ordinarily mixed with water. Sometimes each reveler had a crystal goblet for his own use; other times, each drank from a common cup passed from drinker to drinker by a wine pourer known as the *sáki*.[1] This servant, who played an important role in creating the desired atmosphere, was usually a young boy specially trained to perform his office with flirtatious charm and in accordance with prescribed rules of etiquette. When the function was performed by young girls, they wore their hair short and dressed like boys. The erotic aspect of the *sáki's* contribution to the revel will be discussed in Chapter II.

Although parties did occasionally take place indoors, the favored site was outside on the patio of a palace with gardens, fountains, and canals; on a lawn by the banks of a river; or even on a boat plying the Ebro or the Guadalquivir. The favored time was the night, usually all night, with the drinkers alternately dozing and waking. The experience that they cultivated was a state between waking and sleep, in which the revelers lost their orientation in time and gained a feeling of night infinitely prolonged. Accordingly, Arabic wine poetry has yielded wonderful descriptions of the night sky and meditations on the passage of time that we will take up in Chapter III. The many poems that begin with a call to rise early for drinking are presumably addressed to a sleeping group of revelers, urging them to take up the cup again. This call to the morning cup is often juxtaposed ironically with the muezzin's call to prayer, as in the daring line by Abu Nuwas: "Give me a cup to distract me from the muezzin's call."[2] The idea is familiar to English readers through the opening stanzas of Edward Fitzgerald's *Rubáiyát of Omar Khayyám:*

> Wake! For the sun, who scatter'd into flight
> The Stars before him from the Field of Night
>   Drives Night along with them from Heav'n, and strikes
> The Sultan's Turret with a Shaft of Light.
>
> Before the phantom of False morning died,
> Methought a Voice within the Tavern cried,
>   "When all the Temple is prepared within
> Why nods the drowsy Worshipper outside?"[3]

While the revelers passed the night drinking, nodding, waking, and drinking again, they enjoyed the performances of dancers and singers, either accompanied by an orchestra composed of a variety of musical instruments or accompanying themselves. Both singers and dancers were usually women who performed behind a curtain, or *sitara,* which lent the orchestra its name.

These are the main features of the Arabic wine drinking parties as they are known to us from poetry and anecdotes recorded by medieval chroniclers and biographers.[4] The practice of wine drinking—its setting, timing, customary personnel, and entertainment— as described in the Hebrew poetry of the period is identical to that recorded in Arabic sources. It would seem perfectly reasonable to assume that the Hebrew poetry documents a social reality no less than does the Arabic and that the Andalusian Jewish gentry entertained themselves in exactly the same manner as did the Muslim gentry. That some kind of wine-drinking entertainments occurred among the Jews is clear from Maimonides, who speaks of Jewish "elders" and "pious men" attending wine parties at which secular poems in Arabic and Hebrew were sung.[5]

It is futile to argue that the language and style of the poetry and the reality they describe are merely a literary fashion copied from Arabic poetry, and that therefore they do not necessarily reflect the experience of the poets. The Arabic wine poetry of Spain is itself an imitation, with the same motifs, visual images, situations, and attitudes as the Arabic poetry of the East, where Abu Nuwas (Iraq, c. 747–c. 813) laid down the conventions of the genre.[6] The Spanish Muslims adopted from the aristocracy of the Abbasid empire not only the poetic conventions of wine poetry but also the institution of the wine party itself. The poetry did not exist in isolation from the institution, but was an intimate part of it. If we find the Jews composing wine poetry similar to that of the Arabs, the likelihood is that they were amusing themselves at wine parties similar to those of the Arabs.

Only part of the entertainment at wine parties was in the hands of professional singers, instrumentalists, and dancers. The participants also entertained themselves with conversation about the topics of the day, literature, and, particularly, poetry.[7] They recited and discussed the poems of others, displayed their own compositions, and played improvisational poetic games. It was apparently his skillful extemporaneous imitation of a prosodically complicated *muwashshah* by Moses Ibn Ezra at a social gathering that brought young Judah Halevi to the attention of the elder courtier.[8]

Several examples of improvisatory poetic games are provided by the collection of humorous short fiction in rhymed prose entitled

Tahkemoni, by the thirteenth-century poet and translator Judah al-Ḥarizi:

> . . . In the days of my youth I was in a gathering of scholars, men so clever as to shame the sages and to silence wits. As we were discussing rhetorical speeches and clever figures, weaving poems into robes of honor with golden studs of beauty, a certain man arose among us, a man of witty speech with a mouth that scattered poetic fancies in every direction, boasting that with his verse he could make the hidden clear and the darkness light; that with his speech he could tear the sea to tatters; and that with the flint of his tongue he could shatter rocky crags. One of the best of the youths, a skillful crafter of verses, whose speech was all studded with pearls set in crystal, challenged him, saying:
>
> "If your boast is justified and your speeches are true, come, let us vie, the two of us, in the battle of verse, by making a couplet in partnership. I shall lay the foundation of the house with one verse, and you will make a second verse containing a simile to round off the idea. If you succeed in fulfilling the terms, you will have whatever you request." The old man said: "What you say is fine; I accept the terms you have set."
>
> The youth came forward and sang of . . . the sword:
>
>> "Behold the sword the fighter's hand has drawn,
>> So bright a sightless man could see it flash—"
>
> The old man answered:
>
>> "I thought 'twas lightning gleaming in the sky
>> When high the warrior lifted it to slash." [9]

The youth challenges the old man with verses on the pen, the lute, the horse, the torch, the sachet, the canal, various kinds of trees, and many other objects, including wine. The old man proves so capable in every case that they all shower him with money.

In another story, the terms of the contest require the use of a particular rhetorical device, a very difficult type of pun:

> One of them said to his fellows, "Is there among you anyone who can compose a homonym-poem?" . . . And when a few of them asked him what a homonym poem might be, he said, "Know that a homonym-poem is one in which every verse ends with the same word; the word itself does not change, but the meaning does." When they heard his speech and understood what he was getting at,

they all ran to their battle stations and each man composed what God put in his heart.

There was an old man present who listened in silence, never moving from his place. . . . When he saw that they were laboring without success and didn't really know their craft, he said to them, "Know that you are riding a difficult road, that you are drawing from a deep well, that you are hewing rocks from a hard mountain. If you wish to hear homonym-poems . . . lend your ears to me and hearken to my words. . . ."

There follow twenty-two couplets, not merely ending with homonyms, as required, but beginning with them as well.[10]

Under such circumstances, any handy object could become the subject of an improvisation, so among the mass of extant short Hebrew poems we find epigrams on all sorts of small items, such as apples, goblets, scissors, and pens, besides the items mentioned previously in the first quotation from the *Taḥkemoni*. At wine parties, the wine itself could provide the chief theme for improvisation, as displayed in the following scene from the *Taḥkemoni*:

I came to the house of a wine party and found there a company of youths with goblets gleaming like suns in their hands, which themselves resembled the celestial spheres. Everyone was singing over his goblet and bowl the praise of the wine.

One said: "The world is like a girl, tender and young, and wine is the fluid beneath her tongue. These gardens resemble her cheek and face; these fountains, the eyes that her visage grace."

Another said, "Wine is the herald that promises joy; it banishes untoward thoughts that annoy."

Several other speakers address the subject in the same vein, but, in accordance with the conventions of the *maqama* genre represented by the *Taḥkemoni*, they are soon outdone:

Among them was an older man, who sat on a spot elevated above the others. He kept his eye always on the cup, and somehow always had the goblet at his side. He mocked the speeches he heard the others making: "Alas for the tropes whose pearls are being wasted and whose themes are being desecrated! Is this how wine is praised? Are these its qualities? Besides forgetting its flavor and its savor, you've forgotten its beauty and its favor, its spice and its price, its name and its fame. You have failed to mention its fresh-

WINE

ness, never spent; its fragrance, and its scent . . . its gleam and its color, its jar and its cover, its honey and its treacle, its rains and their trickle, its rivers and their flow, its fire and its glow. All this you have forgotten, and a wrong path you have trodden."

They all said, "If you can praise its delights . . . you will have a share of all the wealth that we possess."[11]

The sheikh goes on to extemporize a speech in rhymed prose and a poem in praise of wine, then another speech and poem about its dangers.

The literary pastimes illustrated by these quotations from the *Tahkemoni* not only demonstrate the intimate connection between poetry and the wine party but also serve to confirm our picture of the atmosphere of such gatherings. The literary forms they use, like all Golden Age Hebrew poetry and its Arabic models, are highly structured, rich in conventional wit, amusing rather than hearty. They are definitely not stein-thumping songs of the "Ninety-nine Bottles of Beer on the Wall" variety. Their delicacy suits the refinement of the world that created them, a world of quiet amusement rather than raucous carousing.

This is not to say that a life of riot was unavailable to medieval Andalusians. As in the Muslim East, there were taverns, especially in towns with a sizable Christian population, where behavior was less decorous than in the refined atmosphere of the court. Alluded to in some of the poetry in classical Arabic, the life of dissipation and uncourtly pleasure has a literary tradition of its own, couched in stylized colloquial Arabic that borrows from romance vocabulary. The chief representative of this tradition is the Arabic poet Ibn Quzman:

> My life is spent in dissipation and wantonness!
> O joy, I have begun to be a real profligate!
> Indeed it is absurd for me to repent
> When my survival without a wee drink would be certain death.
> *Vino, vino!* And spare me what is said;
> Verily, I go mad when I lose my restraint!
> My slave will be freed, my money irretrievably lost
> On the day I am deprived of the cup.
> Should I be poured a double measure or a fivefold one,
> I would most certainly empty it; if not, fill then the *jarrón!*
> Ho! Clink the glasses with us!

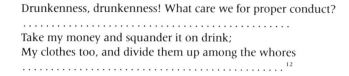

Drunkenness, drunkenness! What care we for proper conduct?

. . . .

Take my money and squander it on drink;
My clothes too, and divide them up among the whores

. . . .[12]

Allusions to the uncourtly life occur also in the *maqama* literature, such as the *Taḥkemoni,* and, rarely, in the love poetry.[13] The greatest classical Arabic poet who devoted much of his work to wine drinking and the associated worldly pleasures, Abu Nuwas, was himself a slightly more dignified representative of this tradition.[14] His poetry was eagerly studied and much imitated, and in many respects became the model of Arabic wine poetry, even of the courtly variety. Many of the standard images, moods, and situations evoked repeatedly in Hispano-Arabic poetry and in the contemporaneous Hebrew poetry can be traced back to his work.

Thematically, two categories of writing appear in the wine poems, both arising from the wine party, its atmosphere and literary diversions. Even when elements of both categories are combined in a single complex poem, they are usually readily distinguishable. Wine poems are either *descriptive* poems, in which the poet describes the wine and the circumstances surrounding its drinking, or they are *meditative* poems, in which the poet muses on the feelings, usually sad ones, that the wine arouses in him.

Descriptive wine poetry deals with the wine's age, its fragrance, clarity, brilliance, and color, and the bubbles at the cup's rim. Wine is compared to fire or the sun because of its appearance and its warming effect on the drinker. The cup is also described: It is usually of crystal, allowing the poets to contrast it with the wine it contains with respect to color, texture, and temperature. Sometimes this juxtaposition of opposites is seen as a miracle. The jug from which the cup is filled, the table on which it is set, the *sáki* who does the serving, and the performers who entertain during the party all attract the poet's attention, as often does the room, patio, or outdoor landscape in which the wine is drunk. These themes and the rhetorical devices applied to them recur frequently, even in the work of the same poet. An excellent, but unfortunately untranslatable, catalogue of these themes and images exists in the book by Moses Ibn Ezra entitled *ʿAnaq,* a collection of homonym-poems on various subjects, much of which is devoted to wine parties.[15]

Meditative themes in wine poetry deal not with the outer world seen by the drinking poet, but with the inner world of his feelings. Just as the descriptive poems dwell rhetorically on contrasting visual juxtapositions, so the meditative poems evoke opposing sensations of joy and sorrow. The luxuriousness of the situation beguiles the poet: the sensuousness of mild intoxication, the music, the fragrances arising from incense and the garden in spring, the voluptuousness of the performers, the comings and goings of the flirtatious *sáki;* and the deeper pleasure of sharing with sophisticated friends who know how to enjoy life an elite, opulent world. Against these sensations, the poet is conscious of another set of feelings: all this beauty will vanish; everything is headed toward destruction; spring arose out of winter and will return to winter just as day and night pursue each other in everlasting alternation. Even friendship does not secure a man against the vicissitudes of time, for friends are as transient as youth and beauty. Thoughts of loss unite meditative and descriptive elements in the fantastic image of the poet, mixing his wine not with water, as was the regular practice, but with tears for friends who are gone: "I drink in horror, and I mix the wine / With tears that from my melting eyes distill."[16]

The two thematic categories are embodied in several different types of poem. By far the most common is the short poem in classical quantitative meter. Because of their brevity and thematic unity, such poems appear to be the kind of verse suitable for recitation at a wine party, whether or not they were actually composed extemporaneously. They may be descriptive or meditative or both, but they never stray far from the wine party, its personnel, artifacts, and surroundings. Short wine poems were composed by all the poets of the period, but two collections deserve particular mention here. Of the ten chapters of Moses Ibn Ezra's book of homonym-poems, two are devoted to themes related to the wine party. Given the limitations inherent in their form, these poems are more ingenious than profound. The many wine poems found in the *dīwān* of Samuel the Nagid, who seems to have devoted more attention to this subject than any other poet of the Golden Age, are far more substantial.[17]

The wine poem also appears frequently as part of the introduction to a longer poem on an entirely different theme. Such complex poems, sometimes called *qasidas,* are descendants of the genre of pre-Islamic Arabic poetry that provided the quantitative meters used by medieval Arabic and Hebrew poets.[18] In the form adopted by Hebrew poets of the Golden Age, such poems string together as a form of introduction several short poems of different genres, such as love, wine, or garden description, before making a transition of an almost formulaic character to the poem's main theme, which is usually a panegyric on a distinguished acquaintance.

Owing to its greater length and thematic complexity, the *qasida* has none of the light, improvised character of the short poem; rather, it is a self-consciously formal ode, demanding the highest standards of refinement. Moses Ibn Ezra and Judah Halevi were masters of the genre. Both composed *qasidas* with introductions containing descriptions of wine parties, but it was Ibn Ezra who made the most of this theme in several monumental poems too weighty for inclusion in this anthology of light verse.[19] Though Western readers tend not to appreciate its hybrid character, this trait was sufficiently attractive to medieval audiences that it was transferred to the *muwashshah.* Many of these poems begin with descriptions of wine or some other theme before shifting by means of a transition verse to panegyric. Though lighter in tone than the *qasidas,* such poems are also excluded from this anthology because their main theme is panegyric.

Like the *Rubáiyát of Omar Khayyám,* the great poem on wine, women, and death cited at the beginning of this chapter, many of the Hebrew wine poems begin with a direct address to an imaginary friend or group of friends, exhorting them to drink. This feature of the poems, which is doubtless partially responsible for their lively tone, is in itself not remarkable, when one considers the social origin of the poems. What is remarkable about it is that, as in the *Rubáiyát,* it is often used to introduce a kind of mock sermon in which the poet urges his auditors to join the party, in the style of a sage adjuring his congregation to a life of piety and good works. This motif has important implications for the genre as a whole. Several of the wine poems in this anthology make use of biblical language and the rhetorical techniques of rabbinic homily in such a way as to give them a tone of parody. Using the language of the synagogue, particularly that of the synagogue preacher, in exhorting to the life customarily denounced by the very speakers with whom it is associated, these poems seem consciously to defy traditional religious values.

This particular mood arose because of a conflict between two opposing principles of life, both commanding the loyalty of cultivated men. On the one hand was the life of this world (*dunya* in Arabic), where temporal things such as political power, material success, and simple physical pleasure are a source of meaning, beauty, and joy. Opposed to this principle was that of the other world (*akhira* in Arabic), the world of the ultimate reality of God and religion, in which the only things that matter are purity of the soul and adherence to God's word, and in the light of which the things of this world are at best empty vanities; at worst, pathways to perdition.

In the culture that produced this poetry, both attitudes were taken seriously by the same men, so that poetry celebrating the pleasures of life and poetry decrying its vanity came from the pens of the same writers. Of course there were pietists and libertines who devoted themselves single-mindedly to one or the other set of values; but the prevailing attitude of Golden Age courtly culture supported both. Sometimes the two occupy separate compartments in the same man's life and work, and sometimes they are uneasily joined. When they come together, as in the poems under discussion, they often produce a nervous kind of humor, for part of the pleasure these men derived from their way of life was of the "stolen waters" variety.

This dichotomy is even clearer in the dominant Muslim society, where not only was the ascetic tendency more deeply rooted in the religious tradition than was the case in Judaism, but also the drinking of wine was actually prohibited by religious law, and even the playing of music was, as in Judaism, religiously problematic.[20] Legal minds exerted themselves to discover loopholes that would permit wine drinking; for example, it was early noted that if *khamr*, the drink interdicted by the Quran, were interpreted as meaning only grape wine, then date wine, or *nabīdh*, would be exempt from the prohibition. Eventually we even find a variety of *nabīdh* being made not from dates but from grapes, and this drink was permitted by many on the grounds that it was not as intoxicating as conventional wine. Such legal fictions did not divert the attention of serious moralists from the real point, that even if wine drinking and its accompanying activities did not necessarily lead to drunkenness, impropriety, lewdness, and homosexuality, they certainly led away from serious thoughts of God and the world to come. Yet in Arabic we find many wine poems that depend for their effect precisely on the poet's and the reader's acknowledgment of the religious impropriety of wine drinking. Abu Nuwas made a career out of shocking his auditors with lines like:

> My proud soul will be content with nothing but the forbidden;
> I do not care when my cup of death will come;
> I have already had my fill of the joys of the cup.[21]

The cultivation of these two conflicting ideals goes back to the very origins of Islam, when the Prophet Mohammad sought to replace the Bedouin tribal culture and its pagan ideals of heroism, military valor (*muruwwa*), and hearty pleasure with the spiritual values of monotheistic religion (*dīn*).[22] Islam never completely succeeded in suppressing the old tribal values, but ended by being superimposed upon them. Thus in the Muslim world, religious and secular mentalities coexisted throughout the Middle Ages.

The secular component in Hispano-Arabic culture needs to be stressed, because the adherence of all the intellectuals of the period to religious tradition, language, and practice tends to obscure for us the extent to which they were able to live by a different set of values. This secular approach to life was inculcated by the educational program itself, with its stress on poetry. Ibn Khaldun, the fourteenth-century historian, while paying lip service to the idea that the Quran is the basis and foundation of all learning, the source of Islam and all the sciences, nevertheless praises the Spanish Muslims for "not stressing the teaching of the Quran more than other subjects." Another medieval authority lauds the Spanish Muslims for teaching their children first Arabic poetry, philology, and arithmetic, and only then the Quran. "How thoughtless are our compatriots in that they teach children the Quran when they are first starting out. They read things they do not understand and work hard at something *that is not as important for them as other matters*" [emphasis mine].[23] With all the prestige of the Quran and the religious sciences, it is no wonder that the educational system of the period "tended to make men of letters rather than men of law."[24] It was thus poetry that largely preserved the memory of tribal life and eventually became the vehicle of medieval secularism.

More decisive for Jewish culture than any specific cultural institution acquired from the Arabs—language, philosophy, social habits, and communal organization—was this centuries-old habit of living in allegiance to two opposing principles, one of which finds its natural expression in poetry and the other in scripture. In the process of acculturation to Hispano-Arabic society, the Jewish aristocracy adapted to Judaism the double life lived by sophisticated Muslims, with its contradictions, ambivalences, and occasional pangs of conscience. Some features of the new style of life were not compatible with the Jewish religious tradition, being contrary to the spirit, if not always to the letter, of religious law; but neither were they fully in accord with the religious law and spirit of the larger society from which they had been adopted. The institution that, for Muslims, most clearly embodied the secular, worldly aspect of their culture was the wine party and its associated entertainments, and it is in the poetry of the wine party that Jews also show us now and again a glimpse of their own troubled conscience.

Besides their religious and moral scruples, shared with the Arabs, about the ideals represented by the wine party, the Jews had another reservation peculiar to themselves. Participation in the pleasures of the dominant culture could be viewed as an act of disloyalty to Jewish national interest. This disloyalty had several aspects. There was a tendency, which never became fully normative but left concrete marks on Jewish life, to view expressions of joy, such as laughing, drinking wine, and eating meat, as inappropriate for any Jew after the destruction of the Temple. Certain ritual observances still reflect this attitude, and from time to time sects have arisen of Jews who devoted their lives to ritual mourning for the fall of Jerusalem.[25] This is the force behind Dunash's question, which we will examine more closely in poem 2:

WINE

> How can we be carefree
> Or raise our cups in glee,
> When by all men are we
> Rejected and despised?

This type of asceticism probably was not taken seriously by individual medieval Jews in their personal lives; but the wine party was a group activity of a particular social class within Judaism, a class that included communal leaders, serious religious thinkers, and bearers of the elite intellectual tradition. Such men may very well have entertained reservations about the propriety of a public life of pleasure.

These reservations were a result not only of loyalty to the Jewish past of suffering and exile. There might also have been a theological reservation, a consideration of the purpose of the continued existence of the Jewish people long after the loss of Jewish sovereignty. Israel had sinned; God had punished her by destroying the Temple and putting an end to the state. Yet instead of destroying the people utterly He had sent them into exile. Was the exile not to be considered a means of expiation? By enduring it in the right spirit they would one day deserve the restoration of God's favor; but the key to salvation was "the right spirit." Surely the luxurious life represented by the wine party must nullify the salutary effect of the life in exile intended by God.[26]

Finally, the Jewish aristocrats, steeped as they were in traditional Jewish lore, must sometimes have looked at their own lives in wonderment, seeing how much they had come to resemble their hosts, the Muslim majority, and their models, the Muslim courtiers. The Jewish courtiers had adopted not only the Arabic language but also the whole way of life that went with it, conscious all the while that the talmudic rabbis had declared it the duty of Jews to safeguard their national identity by shunning the customs and practices of their host peoples. They remembered that the Psalmist had denounced their ancestors with the words: "They mingled with the nations and learned their ways."[27] Even the use of Arabic poetic forms such as quantitative meters and monorhyme came in for this kind of criticism; yet poetry was only the literary expression of a whole way of life that had been borrowed from outsiders.[28] Nor were these outsiders merely unknown foreigners. They were, from the point of view of Jewish tradition, the usurpers of Israel's glory, the conquerors of the Holy Land, the subjugators of the Jewish people. They were Ishmael, the rival of Isaac and the claimant to his title as the archetypal martyr in submission (*islām*, in Arabic) to God's command. They were, in theory at least, the enemy.

Since Hebrew was unknown to the Arabs, it is certain that the Hebrew poetry of the wine party could have been intended only for the amusement of Jewish society. But the high rank attained by men such as Ḥasdai Ibn Shaprut and Samuel the Nagid could have been attained only through integration into the social life of the Muslim courts, and such Jews must sometimes have found themselves participating in entertainments given by Muslim hosts.[29] Here, for example, is the testimony of one of the greatest rabbinic authorities of eleventh-century Iraq, Hai Gaon:

> As to your question about the legal position of one who, in our time [i.e., since the destruction of the Temple], drinks [wine] to the accompaniment of music, especially among non-Jews: he is culpable and to be excommunicated, unless he is a courtier [lit.: he stands before the ruler] and works for the protection of the Jews and trusts himself not to lapse into licentiousness; and unless it is known that at the time [of drinking and listening to music] he is concentrating on the destruction of the Temple, and he is forcing his heart to be sad and not enjoying himself; and unless he listens [to music] only out of deference to the king in order to benefit Israel. For the last hundred years and more there have been in Iraq men in the king's service [lit.: standing at the king's gate] whom the Rabbis permitted such things . . .[30]

In view of the many passing references to Jews by contemporary Arab writers, it seems likely that even Jews lower on the social scale than these exceptional figures may have mixed socially with Muslims. How did such Jews conduct themselves? Did they drink gentile wine, eat gentile food? Were special provisions made for them so that they could take part in the life of the larger world without betraying their religious and national loyalties? In connection with the wine party, some of the halachic problems faced by the Jewish courtiers were doubtless amenable to ingenious solutions. But in the area of sexual relations, the subject of Chapter II, the halachic principles are less tractable.

For the most part, these tensions between the demands of religion and the attraction of the larger society were simply overlooked in the poetry, and poets kept their religion and their social life carefully separated in their work. Sometimes the poets express the tension by bringing the two principles together: We shall see several examples in this chapter. If the dichotomy between the two ways of life is brought to the surface in the wine poetry more often than in poetry on other themes, this is only partly because the Muslim poets, to whom wine was explicitly forbidden, established the conventions of the genre. It is mainly because of the symbolic character of the wine party held in a garden in spring.

Our collection of wine poems begins, appropriately, with a celebration of spring.

·1·

—|—|—|—|—//—|—|—|—

כָּתְנוֹת פַּסִּים / לָבַשׁ הַגַּן / וּכְסוּת רִקְמָה / מַדֵּי דְשָׁאוֹ,

וּמְעִיל תַּשְׁבֵּץ / עָטָה כָל עֵץ / וּלְכָל עַיִן / הֶרְאָה פִלְאוֹ.

כָּל צִיץ חָדָשׁ / לִזְמָן חָדָשׁ / יָצָא שׂוֹחֵק / לִקְרַאת בּוֹאוֹ—

אַךְ לִפְנֵיהֶם / שׁוֹשָׁן עָבַר, / מֶלֶךְ, כִּי עַל / הוּרַם כִּסְאוֹ.

יָצָא מִבֵּין / מִשְׁמַר עָלָיו / וַיְשַׁנֶּה אֶת / בִּגְדֵי כִלְאוֹ.

מִי לֹא יִשְׁתֶּה / יֵינוֹ עָלָיו— / הָאִישׁ הַהוּא / יִשָּׂא חֶטְאוֹ!

משה אבן עזרא

·1·

The garden wears a colored coat,
    The lawn has on embroidered robes,
The trees are wearing checkered shifts,
    They show their wonders to every eye,
And every bud renewed by spring
    Comes smiling forth to greet his lord.
See! Before them marches a rose,
    Kingly, his throne above them borne,
Freed of the leaves that had guarded him,
    No more to wear his prison clothes.
Who will refuse to toast him there?
    Such a man his sin will bear.

Moses Ibn Ezra

·1·

Our first encounter with Andalusian Jewry's conception of the good life occurs, appropriately, in a garden. The scene is revisited in poem after poem: It is spring, and the poet summons the world to drink in celebration of the revival of nature. In this particular poem, the call is given indirectly by means of the general rule enunciated in verse 6: Who will refuse to toast him there? / Such a man his sin will bear. This justly famous piece is actually a cultural manifesto couched in the form of a perfectly crafted descriptive poem.

Of all the lovely sensations that one may experience in a spring-time garden, the poet chooses to describe only those that arise from visual beauty. He imagines the garden dressing up in brightly colored finery in celebration of the new season, embodied in the garden's most flamboyant object, the rose. This rose is conceived as a king to whom the garden pays homage. This metaphor is not merely a passing conceit or a rhetorical flourish, but a central image upon which the whole poem is built. Biblical allusions confirm it repeatedly: "His throne above them borne" (literally: "His throne is lifted high") recalls the words of King David, "The saying of David the son of Jesse / And the saying of the man raised on high."[1] "No more to wear his prison clothes" (literally: "And changed out of his prison clothes") is a quotation from the story of the release of the Judean king Jehoiachin from Babylonian imprisonment.[2] Joseph also changed his clothes upon his release from prison, shortly before Pharoah set him in charge of all of Egypt and had all his subjects shout his acclamation.[3]

If the rose is king, the flowers, trees, and grass of the garden are courtiers, for the "colored coat" worn by the garden is a *ketonet pasim*, the same garment as that worn in his youth by that quintessential courtier Joseph, by King David's daughter Tamar, and by the other princesses of David's court.[4] They are awaiting the arrival of the king, an event that is carefully prepared for by the poem's rhythm. Like all the poems in this book, this poem conforms to the requirements of Andalusian-Hebrew quantitative metrics; unlike the others, it is in a meter that consists entirely of long syllables. Because nearly all of the words in the first three verses have two syllables with the second syllable stressed, the practical effect is that of an accentual rhythm, in the iambic pattern favored by English:

kotnót pasím lavásh hagán
ukhsút riqmá midé dish̓ó

But this pattern is abruptly reversed upon the appearance of the rose in verse 4:

ákh lifnehem shoshan ʿavar
mélekh ki ʿal huram kisʾo

The stresses at the beginnings of the two half-lines are the rhythmic equivalent of the stunning visual impression made by the flamboyant flower: It is the appearance of the rose made audible. The stresses in the translation have been organized in imitation of this effect.

The rose is a dramatic flower; it waits for the end of spring, when the other flowers are in place, to make its entrance: hence the image of a group of courtiers awaiting the imminent return of their sovereign. But the idea of the sovereign carries with it another not readily associated by us with spring, and that is the idea of duty.

The courtiers rejoice at the restoration of their lord, but their lord expects more of them than mere joy; he expects an act of allegiance, an affirmation of his courtiers' fealty. The force of this political metaphor would have been acutely felt by the courtier-rabbis of Moses Ibn Ezra's circle. King Rose has a demand to make of his followers: In allegiance to him, they are all to drink wine in the garden, and whoever abstains will bear his guilt.

This threat against the dissenter may seem vague, but to the poet's Bible-educated audience it was sufficiently specific. "Such a man his sin will bear" is the warning attached by the Bible to the laws of the Passover offering, in a passage that stresses the obligation of the individual to share in the communal celebration. Of the man who neglects the Passover sacrifice scripture says: "that soul shall be cut off from his people . . . that man shall bear his sin"[5]; "cut off from the community of servants of the rose" is our poet's implicit threat for the man who neglects this Golden Age springtime observance. The punishment of the man who fails to celebrate the renewal of the garden is that he will have no share in the garden. This secular cup of salvation is a ritual of communion with a social class that derived the meaning of its existence from beauty. He who excludes himself will have to live with being excluded. His sin is its own punishment, an idea that is inherent in biblical Hebrew usages of words for sin.[6]

Our opening wine poem thus goes further than most of the poems that we will be reading in this section. It does not simply recommend a hedonistic style of life rooted in the *carpe diem* motif. It does not ask the audience merely to think about life, its brevity and vicissitudes, and to choose pleasure while it may. It makes demands, using the political vocabulary of allegiance, loyalty, and rebellion, and the religious language of sin and punishment, to enunciate a new rule of life.[7]

‒‒‒‒‒∪|‒|‒‒‒‒‒∪

2

וְאֹמַר "אַל תִּישָׁן! / שְׁתֵה יֵין יָשָׁן—

עֲלֵי מֹר עִם שׁוֹשָׁן / וְכֹפֶר וַאֲהָלִים

בְּפַרְדֵּס רִמּוֹנִים / וְתָמָר וּגְפָנִים

וְנִטְעֵי נַעֲמָנִים / וּמִינֵי הָאֶשְׁלִים,

וְרֶגֶשׁ צִנּוֹרִים / וְהֶמְיַת כִּנּוֹרִים

עֲלֵי פֶה הַשָּׁרִים / בְּמִנִּים וּנְבָלִים,

וְשָׁם כָּל עֵץ מוּנָף / יְפֵה פְּרִי עָנָף

וְצִפּוֹר כָּל כָּנָף / יְרַנֵּן בֵּין עָלִים,

וְיֶהְגּוּ הַיּוֹנִים / כְּהוֹגִים נְגוּנִים,

וְהַתּוֹרִים עוֹנִים / וְהוֹמִים כַּחֲלִילִים.

וְנִשְׁתֶּה בַעֲרוּגוֹת / בְּשׁוֹשַׁנִּים סוּגוֹת,

וְנָנִיס הַתּוּגוֹת / בְּמִינֵי הַלּוּלִים,

וְנֹאכַל מַמְתַּקִּים / וְנִשְׁתֶּה מְזָרְקִים

וְנִנְהַג כַּעֲנָקִים / וְנִשְׁתֶּה בִסְפָלִים,

וְאָקוּם בַּבְּקָרִים / אֲנִי לִשְׁחֹט פָּרִים

בְּרִיאִים נִבְחָרִים / וְאֵילִים וַעֲגָלִים,

וְנִמְשַׁח שֶׁמֶן טוֹב / וְנַקְטִיר עֵץ רָטֹב.

בְּטֶרֶם יוֹם קָטֹב / יְבוֹאֻנוּ נַשְׁלִים".

גְּעַרְתִּיהוּ "דֹּם, דֹּם, / עֲלֵי זֹאת אֵיךְ תְּקֹדָם—

וּבֵית קֹדֶשׁ וַהֲדֹם / אֱלֹהִים לַעֲרֵלִים!

בְּכִסְלָה דִבַּרְתָּ / וְעַצְלָה בָחַרְתָּ

וְהֶבֶל אָמַרְתָּ / כְּלֵצִים וּכְסִילִים,

וְעָזַבְתָּ הֶגְיוֹן / בְּתוֹרַת אֵל עֶלְיוֹן

וְתָגִיל — וּבְצִיּוֹן / יְרוּצוּן שׁוּעָלִים.

וְאֵיךְ נִשְׁתֶּה יַיִן / וְאֵיךְ נָרִים עַיִן—

וְהָיִינוּ אַיִן / מְאוּסִים וּגְעוּלִים!"

דונש בן לברט

·2·

There came a voice: "Awake!
Drink wine at morning's break.
'Mid rose and camphor make
A feast of all your hours,

'Mid pomegranate trees
And low anemones,
Where vines extend their leaves
And the palm tree skyward towers,

Where lilting singers hum
To the throbbing of the drum,
Where gentle viols thrum
To the plash of fountains' showers.

On every lofty tree
The fruit hangs gracefully.
And all the birds in glee
Sing among the bowers.

The cooing of the dove
Sounds like a song of love.
Her mate calls from above—
Those trilling, fluting fowls.

We'll drink on garden beds
With roses round our heads.
To banish woes and dreads
We'll frolic and carouse.

Dainty food we'll eat.
We'll drink our liquor neat,
Like giants at their meat,
With appetite aroused.

When morning's first rays shine
I'll slaughter of the kine
Some fatlings; we shall dine
On rams and calves and cows.

Scented with rich perfumes,
Amid thick incense plumes,
Let us await our dooms,
Spending in joy our hours."

I chided him: "Be still!
How can you drink your fill
When lost is Zion hill
To the uncircumcised.

You've spoken like a fool!
Sloth you've made your rule.
In God's last judgment you'll
For folly be chastised.

The Torah, God's delight
Is little in your sight,
While wrecked is Zion's height,
By foxes vandalized.

How can we be carefree
Or raise our cups in glee,
When by all men are we
Rejected and despised?"

Dunash ben Labrat

·2·

The presentation of arguments for and against a given proposition was a skill cultivated by Arab rhetoricians as it had been among the Greeks, and authors occasionally turned this practice into a poetic form. An idea is presented to the reader in an attractive way, leading him to accept it as the poet's own point of view. Just when the reader is comfortable with it, the poet pulls it away from him in an unexpected retraction. The effect of the poem comes from the manipulation of the reader's attitude toward the proposition, and it is the very conventional nature of the thematics of this literature that makes such manipulation possible.

An excellent example is the opening of a panegyric by Judah Halevi.[1] "Let not the world seduce you with its vanity," warns the poet; and to help the reader recognize the world's temptations and avoid them, he devotes no fewer than twenty-one long, lush verses to their description. Many of the items described are the same as the ones in our poem: the garden in spring, its trees and fountain, the wine drunk by the revelers, and the wine cups. The description is so long, detailed, and enthusiastic that it takes on a life of its own, so that the poem's opening warning is completely forgotten until the speaker breaks in with the remark, "This is the sort of thing the world has set before me that I might forget its troubles." In what follows, these pleasures are denounced as evanescent and delusive, culminating in the words, "there is no delight in beauty," sweeping away with an abstract and categorical denial the mood and tone so elaborately established in the beginning.

Far less sophisticated in every aspect of technique, the present poem uses a similar overall method. Its rejection of the pleasures of the senses has, however, a different cause. Halevi has in mind the reader's personal welfare: It is prudent to distrust a world that is sure to betray you. Dunash has in mind the national dilemma: It is *immoral* to indulge in pleasure when the Jewish people is in exile. Along the way, the luxuries available to the medieval Jewish aristocrat are described in such enthusiastic detail that the medieval copyist to whose assiduousness we owe the preservation of the poem understood this to be the main theme. To the text of the poem he attached the following preface, summarizing the first part of the poem and completely passing over the retraction:

WINE

Another poem by ben Labrat on the kinds of drinking in the evening and in the morning and on [doing so] without letup, in a light meter, accompanied by instruments and the sound of canals and the humming of strings and the chirping of birds in the trees, and the fragrance of incense, all of which he described in the presence of Ḥasdai Ibn Shaprut. . .[2]

Some believe that Dunash put his heart into the descriptive part of the poem, with its exuberant detail and energetic tone, and that the retraction, like the last two verses of Ecclesiastes, is a mere nod toward traditionalists added to make the poet respectable. Others say that it is the retraction, with its simple, straightforward, heartfelt language, and not the descriptive part, a mere display of virtuosity with its metrical and lexical gaucheries, that is the real point of the poem. My feeling is that Dunash really believed in both parts of his poem, and that he used this particular form in order to expose his own conflicted feelings about the very way of life so forcefully advocated in the preceding poem.

Dunash belonged to the original group of literary pioneers who rather self-consciously began the Golden Age in the time of Ḥasdai Ibn Shaprut; it was he who devised the prosodic principles that made possible the imitation of the formal characteristics of Arabic poetry. To this generation, the new poetry was part of a new and exciting way of life that might, however, lead away from traditional Jewish concerns and traditional cultural cohesiveness. It must have felt as if the voice of the secular culture of the Arabic courts were actually calling to the Jews to share in its pleasures; and the Jewish grandees, or some of them, listened to the traditionalist inner voices warning them against forgetting their people—and joined the party. The next 200 years were spent trying to find the balance between the prestige, glamour, and attractiveness of Hispano-Arabic culture and the demands of Jewish loyalty.

This poem, written at the very beginning of the period, lays out the problem of conscience as clearly as any other document of the period, and leaves it unresolved. The invitation is neither explicitly accepted nor declined.

The poem is composed in a prosodic pattern known as "Dunash's meter." This form divides each verse into four lines, rhyming aaax, bbbx, and so forth, the x rhyme continuing unchanged throughout the poem. Whereas internal rhyme occurs as a special device in Arabic poetry, it never occurs as an intrinsic part of the form except in certain non-classical genres such as the *muwashshaḥ*. The meter associated with this particular verse pattern, though quantitative, is also not a classical pattern, the ratio between long and short syllables being far higher than is normal, so that the rhythm is unnaturally even. Though every important Hebrew poet made occasional use of "Dunash's meter," it was not destined to become an important form in Hebrew; it represents an experimental stage in the adaptation of Arabic prosody to Hebrew, and doubtless sounded like doggerel to ears accustomed to the long, grave, lines of Arabic verse. In the translation I have attempted to convey this effect, although I was unable to maintain the x rhyme throughout the poem.

WINE

·3·

‏— — — ◡│— ◡∕∕— — ◡│— — ◡

עֲלֵיכֶם לְפוֹעַלְכֶם לְיַשֵּׁר פְּעוּלֵיכֶם —
וְלָכֶם יְהִי עָלָיו לְשַׁלֵּם גְּמוּלֵיכֶם.
וְאַל בַּעֲבוֹדָתוֹ תְּבַלּוּ יְמוֹתֵיכֶם,
אֲבָל עֵת עֲשׂוּ לָאֵל וְעִתִּים עֲשׂוּ לָכֶם.
תְּנוּ לוֹ חֲצִי הַיּוֹם וְחֶצְיוֹ לְמַעֲשֵׂיכֶם
וְאַל תִּתְּנוּ פוּגַת לְיַיִן בְּלֵילֵיכֶם!
וְכַבּוּ מְאוֹר הַנֵּר — וְאוֹרוּ בְכוֹסֵיכֶם,
וְקוּצוּ בְקוֹל שָׁרִים — וְשִׁירוּ בְנִבְלֵיכֶם.
וְאִם אֵין בְּקֶבֶר שִׁיר וְחֶמֶר וְחָבֵר — הוֹי
פְּתָאִים, יְהִי זֶה חֶלְקְכֶם מֵעֲמָלֵיכֶם!

שמואל הנגיד

·3·

Your debt to God is righteously to live,
     And His to you, your recompense to give.
Do not wear out your days in serving God;
     Some time devote to Him, some to yourself.
To Him give half your day, to work the rest;
     But give the jug no rest throughout the night.
Put out your lamps! Use crystal cups for light.
     Away with singers! Bottles are better than lutes.
No song, nor wine, nor friend beneath the sward—
     These three, O fools, are all of life's reward.

Samuel the Nagid

·3·

The tone of the opening sentence is rendered rather pompous by the use of legal idioms involving debts and credits, and by a play on words not evident in the translation. The sentence literally means: "You owe *him who made* you to make your *deeds* righteous," the two italicized phrases deriving from the same root. This verbal play suggests an ethical balance that justifies the creditor-debtor imagery: as God executed *his* work in creating you (the auditor) with integrity, so it behooves you to do *your* work, live your life, with integrity. Thus the theme of the poem is shown at the outset to be the determination of the exact balance of responsibility between God and man; at which, the auditor settles in for a sermon.

The judicial style continues unbroken in the second hemistich, but the theologically outrageous notion that God owes man anything at all turns the tone to parody; we realize that the poet has marshaled all this sententiousness in order to advise us to devote as much of our lives to pleasure as we dare.

"Some time devote to Him, some to yourself" sounds like an even division of man's time between the secular and the sacred, but actually the ratio works out as less favorable to God. A literal translation of verse 2 would be: "Make time for God and time*s* for yourselves."[1] This seemingly insignificant fluctuation between singular and plural in parallel passages is the kind of textual irregularity that attracted the attention of the Talmudists. To such irregularities they often attached apparently unrelated ideas, sometimes of far-ranging importance. It is the kind of fine point that would have been second nature to an expert Talmudist like the Nagid. Forced though it may seem to a modern reader of Western poetry, it is probably correct to interpret this line as hinting at a one third for God, two thirds for pleasure division of one's time. The verse, in fact, parodies a specific passage in the Talmud, in which two rabbis debate the correct allocation of time on feast days to feasting and study.[2]

The ratio is reduced further still in verse 3. If the auditor thought that the poet was recommending that half one's time be allotted to God and half to oneself, he is now reminded that nighttime was not included in the equation. The night, dead time to respectable folk (like the sober reader himself), is assigned completely to pleasure: God is left with a mere fraction of our time.

If any doubt remains as to where a man should concentrate his efforts, the rhyme scheme of the poem provides a strong indication. The formal rhyme, which occurs at the end of each verse, is *l*(vowel)*khem*. *Khem* is a pronomial suffix meaning "you." In the form *lakhem* it means "for you," "for yourselves," and this form actually occurs at the end of verse 2. But the suffix *khem* also appears at the end of every hemistich in the poem but one, so that drumming in our ears we hear "you . . . you . . . you."

The play on the two meanings of the word "rest" in verse 3 is not in the Hebrew. I have used it to suggest the various kinds of rhetorical balancing that appear in the original and which are so bound to the language that I could not reproduce them in English. Plays on homonyms and near homonyms (*tajnīs*) were very much in vogue in the Arabic poetry that was current when the Jews were re-learning the craft of poetry. Such devices are important to this particular poem because they mimic rhetorically the images of just measure, balance, and equivalence that permeate it. The same function is served by the latent pun in the second half of verse 4, which literally means: "Reject the voice of singers, but sing with your wineskins"; the pun is on the word *nevel*, which, besides meaning "wineskins" also is the name of a musical instrument. The word play thus confirms the substitution recommended in both hemistichs.

The fun in this poem arises from a kind of flirtation with blasphemy quite in keeping with the Nagid's personality. In his sincere piety, he sometimes shows an inclination to depict God as a prince or a more powerful courtier with whom one can enter into agreements and bargains, and with whom one's relationship depends on a balance of favors bestowed and services rendered.[3]

For "wine, women, and song," our trinity of the good life, the poet has "wine, friend, and song," with the conviviality of male society replacing the eroticism of many other poems. This stress on friendship and conviviality is found in poems of other genres as well, and fear of its loss is a source of anxiety second only to fear of death. Moses Ibn Ezra's laments for his fate as a wanderer in Christian Spain, far from his circle of Andalusian Jewish courtiers, are only a special case, a general theme expressed through a particular biography.

WINE

·4·

—|—∪—|—∪—∪|—|—∪—|—//—|—∪—|—∪—∪|—|—∪—

אִם תְּאַוֶּה, כְּמוֹ נָאוֶה לְנַסֵּךְ / יֵין שְׂמָחוֹת, שְׁמַע הֲגִיגֵי לְשׁוֹנִי:

אוֹרְךָ אֶת נְתִיב שְׂשׂוֹנִים, וְאִם לֹא / תַּאֲמִין לִי, אֲחִי אֲנָחוֹת וְעֹנִי,

כִּי חֲמִשָּׁה יְמַלְּאוּ הַלְּבָבוֹת / בַּשְׂמָחוֹת וְהֵם יְנִיסוּן יְגוֹנִי:

יַעֲלַת־חֵן וְגַן וְיַיִן וְרִגְשַׁת / מֵי נְחָלִים וְשִׁיר יְעִירוּן שְׂשׂוֹנִי.

שמואל הנגיד

·4·

If you're like me, and want to pour the wine of joy,
    Hear what I have to say.
I'll teach you pleasure's way, though you don't want to hear,
    You friend of sighs and pain.
Five things there are that fill the hearts of men with joy,
    And put my grief to flight:
A pretty girl, a garden, wine, the water's rush
    In a canal, and song.

Samuel the Nagid

·4·

The three essentials of the good life enumerated in the preceding poem are here replaced by five. The first, a pretty girl, displaces the all-male circle of friends with a quiet eroticism; song comes last, the culmination of the list, or the vehicle for the expression and preservation of the other elements of the good life. Between the girl and the song come the three elements that together provide the setting: a wine party in a garden adorned with water channels.

This poem differs from the preceding one in its more personal, confidential tone; "take it from me, my friend" would be our idiomatic equivalent. In both poems, the speaker presents himself as a man of greater wisdom and experience, imparting to a silent, less sophisticated interlocutor his counsel on the good life. A rhythmic peculiarity in this poem further distinguishes the speaker's tone from that of the mock-preacher of poem 3.

The rhythmic effect of Hebrew quantitative meter derives from the balancing of the two halves of the verse. Ordinarily, the balancing of metrically equal hemistichs is matched by syntactic balancing, sometimes in the form of parallelism, sometimes in other ways, but usually the end of the first hemistich corresponds to the end of a clear syntactic unit. Exceptions to the rule occur either because of metrical necessity or for the sake of some particular effect intended by the poet; they are sporadic, because their effect depends on the background of a dependable rise and fall.[1] Yet in this poem, *every verse* has hemistich enjambment. That this is not an accident is proved by the fact that the number of run-on syllables is the same in all four verses, i.e., four syllables, constituting, in this meter, a whole metric foot. It is hard to imagine how the auditor would experience the rhythm of such a structure. The first line must have sounded limp and shapeless. The second might have given the auditor the feel of the rhythm, enabling him to follow it, but the poem would continue to sound eccentric, and the auditor would be waiting for a correction of the imbalance.[2] At the recitation's close, either he would consider the poem a failure or he would accept the rhythmic eccentricity as a form of expression appropriate to a slightly tipsy speaker; this, I think, is what the poet intended.

‏— — ‏◡ ‏— — ‏— ‏| — — — ‏◡ ‏| / — ‏| — — — ‏◡ ‏| — — — ‏◡

יְדִידִי, כָּל שְׁנוֹתֶיךָ תְּנוּמוֹת / וְטוֹבָתָם וְרָעָתָם חֲלוֹמוֹת,
וְעַל כָּכָה אֱטֹם אֹזֶן וְעַיִן / עֲצֹם — יִתֵּן לְךָ אֵל תַּעֲצוּמוֹת! —
וְהַנִּיחַ דְּבָרִים נַעֲלָמִים / בְּעוֹלָמָךְ לְמֵבִין תַּעֲלוּמוֹת,
וְהַשְׁקֵנִי יְשִׁישָׁה בָּאֲשִׁישָׁה / בְּכַף עַלְמָה מְטִיבָה בַּעֲלָמוֹת
יְשָׁנָה מִן יְמוֹת אָדָם, וְאִם לֹא — / חֲדָשָׁה מִן יְמֵי אִישׁ הָאֲדָמוֹת!
יְהִי רֵיחָהּ כְּרֵיחַ מֹר וְקָנֶה / וּמַרְאֶהָ — כְּמַרְאֵה פָז וְרָאמוֹת,
כְּיַיִן דָּוִד הֱכִינוּהוּ מְלָכוֹת / בְּנִקְיוֹן וּפִילַגְשִׁים נְעִימוֹת,
וְיוֹם הֻנַּח בְּגֶבֶל — שָׁר בְּצַחוֹת / וְצַחְצָחוֹת עֲלֵי נִבְלוֹ יְרִימוֹת
וְשָׂח "כָּזֶה יְהִי אָצוּר וְשָׁמוּר / וְאָסוּר בַּחֲבִיּוֹת הַחֲתוּמוֹת
לְכָל שׁוֹתֶה בְּלֵב טוֹב מֵי עֲנָבִים / וְאוֹחֵז כּוֹס בְּיָדַיִם חֲכָמוֹת,
וְשׁוֹמֵר דָּת בְּקֹהֶלֶת כְּתוּבָה / וְחָרֵד מִתְּלָאוֹת אַחֲרֵי מוֹת".

שמואל הנגיד

·5·

My friend, we pass our lives as if in sleep;
      Our pleasures and our pains are merely dreams.
But stop your ears to all such things, and shut
      Your eyes—may Heaven grant you strength!—
Don't speculate on hidden things; leave that
      To God, the Hidden One, whose eye sees all.

But send the lass who plays the lute
      To fill the cup with coral drink,
Put up in kegs in Adam's time,
      Or else just after Noah's flood,
A pungent wine, like frankincense,
      A glittering wine, like gold and gems,
Such wine as concubines and queens
      Would bring King David long ago.

The day they poured that wine into the drum,
      King David's singer Jerimoth would strum
And sing: "May such a wine as this be kept
      Preserved and stored in sealed-up kegs and saved
For all who crave the water of the grape,
      For every man who holds the cup with skill,
Who keeps the rule Ecclesiastes gave,
      Revels, and fears the tortures of the grave."

Samuel the Nagid

WINE

Here is yet another wine poem in which the speaker assumes the tone of sage counselor. The opening sententious reflection on life's insubstantiality, the closing admonition to live in accordance with the precepts of scripture, and the allusions to biblical personages in the body of the poem make it a parody of pietistic verse.

The Hebrew words translated as "all such things" in verse 2 do not have a very definite antecedent, but given the straight-faced gnomic opening of the poem, it seems to be the "pleasures and the pains" of the material world that the listener is advised to ignore. The next line suggests intellectual self-control as the proper counterpart to physical asceticism, a view with surprisingly deep roots in Jewish pietism.[1] But when verse 4 makes us aware of the poem's true message, the ironic character of the preceding verses becomes apparent. Verse 2 is really advising the listener to censor bothersome reflections such as that which opens the poem. If life is nothing but sleep, then sleep! Leave the thinking to God, and drink up.[2]

The alliterations in verse 4 of the Hebrew poem are metrically organized to give the open statement of the poet's intention a different rhythm from the verses that precede and follow: a prosodic complement to the turn-about in theme. To imitate the effect I altered the meter in the English version, restoring the longer lines approximately where the special effect fades, as the poet, having placed the reader in the new sphere of unambiguous sensuality, restores the poem's basic rhythm.

Although poetic descriptions of wine customarily deal with its fragrance, color, age, and effect upon the drinker, the descriptive portion of this poem, beginning with verse 4, focuses on the wine's age and only touches on the other themes. It was traditional to invent the most absurd hyperboles regarding the age of the wine. This practice the Nagid has put in the service of his parody by associating the age of the wine with biblical characters, just as a preacher might draw upon the exempla of great men of old.

This hyperbolic claim does not originate with the Nagid, nor is it of Jewish origin; the eighth-century Arabic poet Abu Nuwas describes wine as coming from the age of Adam, Eve, Seth, and Noah.[3] But the Nagid put his personal stamp upon the biblical motif by singling out King David as the model drinker. King David is named both as a measure of the wine's antiquity and because he represents a particular social model, providing the imagination with an ideal setting for drinking wine; no fewer than four verses are devoted to a speech by one of his courtiers that makes wine drinking into a moral legacy bequeathed by this noble king to future generations of discerning men.

Medieval Hebrew poets loved to allude to out-of-the-way passages from the Bible; able to rely on the audience's rote knowledge of scripture, they could even draw upon the "begats" of Genesis and Chronicles for whimsical effects.[4] Here the Nagid has outdone himself in obscurity, choosing as King David's spokesman a biblical personage that even a medieval rabbi might have been slow to identify.

Jerimoth was the fifth of the fourteen sons of Heman, who was one of three Levites whom David appointed with their sons to serve as Temple singers.[5] Mentioned only once in the Bible, in the midst of the stupefying list of names comprising Chapters 23 through 27 of I Chronicles, Jerimoth (as well as his thirteen brothers and numerous cousins) went unmentioned in the Jewish literature of the next 1300 years until revived by Samuel the Nagid, still as a musician, but with a distinctly secular function.

Although his sermon on wine-bibbing derives a tone of mock authority from his sacerdotal profession, Jerimoth seems to combine his role as a clergyman with that of court poet. The Nagid must have fancied King David and the members of his entourage to have lived like contemporary Andalusian princes; in his imagination, the biblical Levite stood in for the poet or singing girl, whose songs celebrated the way of life epitomized by the Andalusian wine party. The Nagid repeatedly lays claim, through his Levitic ancestry, to membership in the Jewish aristocracy and a hereditary gift for poetry—a status equivalent to that of a pure-blooded descendant of Bedouins in medieval Andalusia.[6]

Even more to the point, the Nagid often compares himself to King David, especially in those poems that reflect seriously on his career. In moments of self-doubt, he looked to David—like himself, a man of God with bloody hands—as the biblical paradigm for his own career as statesman, warrior, and poet. David became his model, patron, and vindication: "They ask: 'Should *you* extol the Lord on high' / I say: 'The David of the age am I!'"[7]

The Nagid has thus placed his role model, King David, at a wine party of the Andalusian type, listening to the Nagid's Levitical ancestor Jerimoth singing in praise of the wine and the drinkers. Jerimoth's song, in fact, speaks of wine drinking as the moral legacy of King David's reign. Pietist that he is, he cites biblical authority, saying that the wine being laid up in David's time is to be kept for a later generation of men who will be true to the rule of Ecclesiastes. Although he neglects to tell us which of the many rules of life propounded by Ecclesiastes he has in mind, verses 10 and 11 imply that he is thinking of a passage that commends mixing revelry with piety. Ecclesiastes 11 : 9 fits the purpose admirably:

> Rejoice, young man, in your youth
> And let your heart cheer you in the days of your youth,
> And walk in the ways of your heart
> And in the sight of your eyes
> But know that for all these things
> God will bring you into judgment.[8]

As in so many poems of the Golden Age, part of the wit lies in the overlapping of Jewish and Arabic religious and secular motifs. The secular stock motif here is the antiquity of the wine and the image of cobweb-covered jars sealed generations ago. When this motif is put into Hebrew, especially in the context of a mock sermon delivered by a biblical divine and supported by allusion to a biblical prooftext, it must have reminded his listeners of a theme from a completely different sphere. Steeped in traditional Jewish lore, they would recall the legend of the wine laid up by God for the banquet of the righteous in the world to come.[9] It may seem surprising that the Nagid tempers his recommendation of a life of revelry with thoughts of the grave and the last judgment. Perhaps he is alluding to the talmudic idea that a person will be judged after his death for pleasures forgone in life.[10] I rather think that the ideal drinker is a man as complex as himself, who lives in both the profane and sacred worlds, and who drinks as if there were to be no final judgment—though he knows there is. The serious drinker in Golden Age poetry is more complex than his companions, as we shall have several occasions to observe. Ambivalence is part of the aristocratic experience of the Golden Age.

$$-\ -\ \cup\ |\ -\ -\ \cup\ |\ -\ -\ \cup\ |\ |\ -\ \cup\ |\ -\ -\ \cup\ |\ -\ -\ \cup\ |$$

יְדִידִי, קוּם! כְּבָר אָסְרוּ אֲשִׁישׁוֹת / בְּבוֹר נוּמָה לְכָל עוֹיֵן וּפוֹקֵד
וְאֵין עִמִּי לְבַד שׁוֹתֶה בְלֵב טוֹב / עֲלֵי נֵצֶת סְמָדַר לַח וְשָׁקֵד,
וְעֶלֶם סָב וּמַשְׁקֶה כוֹס, וְעֶלֶם / לְהָרִיק הַחֲבִיּוֹת רָן וְשׁוֹקֵד,
וְכַף עֹפֶר בְּעֵט מֵאֵין דְּיוֹ עַל / פְּנֵי כִנּוֹר כְּכַף כּוֹתֵב וְנוֹקֵד.
וְהָאָרֶץ בְּעֵינֵינוּ כְּעַלְמָה / מְשַׂחֶקֶת וְהָעוֹלָם כְּרוֹקֵד —
וְשָׁמַיִם כְּחַיִל נָם בְּלַיִל / וְכָל אִישׁ שָׁם לְעֻמַּת אָהֳלוֹ קֵד.

שמואל הנגיד

·6·

Wake friend! The watchers with their sullen looks
     Are bound by wine and cast in slumber's pit,
But I am still awake 'mid vines in bloom,
     With two or three who know what drinking is.
The *sáki* makes the rounds, another boy
     Runs back and forth to empty out the kegs.
A fawn is strumming with her quill, like one
     Who writes and then goes back to dot the I's.
The world is smiling at us like a girl,
     And all the universe appears to dance.
The sky is like a troop asleep at night,
     Each soldier with a fire beside his tent.

Samuel the Nagid

·6·

Who are the "watchers" whose slumber affords the poet the opportunity to rouse his sleeping friend? The Hebrew word ʿoyen, related to the word for "eye," means someone who watches another with hostile intent; such "watchers" are part of the standard cast of characters in love poetry, corresponding to the Arabic raqib and the troubadours' lauzenjador and gardador, whom lovers must beware. In the social world presupposed by the poetry, they may be blackmailers, idle gossips, or malicious troublemakers, all of whom could endanger the relationship, lives, or reputation of the lovers by revealing what they know. But in a larger sense, they stand for conventional disapproval, the forces of society that work against the relationship and thus against love itself. Here they are participants in a wine party, but they are not true devotees, not the hearties to whom Jerimoth dedicated King David's vintage. They are conventional drinkers, the kind of people for whom the soporific power of the liquor is stronger than the contemplative pleasures that keep the poet and his real friends awake. To the poet and his circle, they are "the others," who in a later age would be labeled Philistines.

This poem combines elements of the preaching style of the preceding poems with the descriptive character of the following selections. The first verse with its drowsing topers and the last with its tenting troops provide a static background to a scene of continuous, graceful, and largely circular motion. Drinkers customarily sat in a circle, and the poem describes the sáki moving around the circle with the cup.[1] The motion of the other serving boy, whose task is to fill the goblet from the keg, is if not circular at least periodic. The movement of the lute player, here called a fawn (a conventional appellation for a beautiful youth, to be discussed in the introduction to Chapter II), is of greater interest to the poet than her music. The circles described by her arm as she alternately strums and plucks remind him of a scribe writing; the scribe is probably not writing Hebrew, with its bare disconnected consonants, but Arabic, whose flowing alphabet is sprinkled with diacritical points, which he always fills in after writing the graceful flourish at the word's end.

From these small inner circles, the poet contemplates the wider circles of the earth and the sky. An army encamped at night may well be seen as a hostile group sleeping in a circle; thus the cosmic environment, by the end of the poem, has assumed some of the threatening character of the social environment described in its beginning. Not only society, but also life itself, is the enemy of tranquillity and beauty. But this sad thought, underlying all the finest wine poetry, is only implicit in the poem's imagery. The poet's mood is far from the self-pity that sometimes spoils poems of this genre. It is a moment of peace that our poet has "photographed" verbally; we shall encounter the weightier developments of his train of thought in Chapter III.

·7·

—— — ∪ | — — — ∪ | — — — ∪ | / — — ∪ | — — ∪ | — — — ∪

שְׁתֵה אָחִי וְהַשְׁקֵנִי, עֲדֵי כִי / בְּיַד הַכּוֹס יְגוֹן לִבִּי אֲמַגֵּן,

וְאִם אָמוּת לְעֵינֶיךָ — מְהֵרָה / תְּחַיֵּנִי כְּנַגֵּן הַמְנַגֵּן!

משה אבן עזרא

·7·

Drink up, my friend, and pour for me, that I
    May to the cup surrender all my pain.
And if you see me dying, tell the boy,
    "Revive him! Quick! Take up your lute again."

Moses Ibn Ezra

The sorrow implicit in the preceding poem is made explicit in this epigram. Wine drinking provides the positive pleasure of revelry as well as the negative pleasure of forgetfulness. But forgetting is a kind of death, and the poet is very anxious not to lose contact with his feelings: "For shade to shade will come too drowsily, / And drown the wakeful anguish of the soul."[1] To keep himself awake and feeling, the poet has need of his companion, a friend both loyal and hearty, though less sensitive than he to either pleasure or pain.

The poem is lent epigrammatic force by the allusion, in the last two words, to the Prophet Elisha, who ordered that a musician be brought to play for him in order to arouse him to prophesy: "As the musician played . . . the hand of the Lord came upon him."[2] Since a modern English reader would not be likely to catch the reference, I have sacrificed it in the translation for the sake of the rhyme; but Ibn Ezra's audience would not have missed it. The suggestion of a connection between prophecy and music would have greatly interested intellectuals like Moses Ibn Ezra, who liked to speculate on the sources of poetic inspiration. One of the themes of Ibn Ezra's book on poetic theory is the parallelism between prophecy in the Bible and poetry in Arabic culture.[3] From Arabic works on the theory of poetry Ibn Ezra was certainly familiar with the idea that music can induce a special state of inspiration in the poet;[4] it is likely that he would have seen the story of Elisha as the biblical equivalent of this idea. Although Ibn Ezra ultimately rejects the view that the spiritual power of prophecy is the same as that of poetry, he certainly sees the two arts as being related. This idea was not unique to him, but was current among Andalusian intellectuals.

Hearing the allusion to Elisha's minstrel, Ibn Ezra's audience would understand the image of dying and reviving not merely as a hyperbolic description of the speaker's ecstasy but also as a metaphoric expression connecting the poet's sorrow and joy with his own creativity. Commonplace as this idea is to us, it is little mentioned by medieval Hebrew poets, who tended to stress the element of craftsmanship. Moses Ibn Ezra says elsewhere of those who had plagiarized his verses by inserting them in their own poems:

"Never will they be able to compete with my verse / Until with their own feet they cross the river of my tears."[5]

Our epigram was not intended to illuminate the relationship between poetry and prophecy or the emotional sources of poetic inspiration; it merely toys with these weighty problems. It is an "exquisite trifle" of a kind much appreciated in its time.

·8·

∪—∣∪—∣—∪—∣∪—∣—∪∪∣∪—∣—∪—∣∪—∣—∪

אֱהִי כֹפֶר לְעֹפֶר קָם בְּלַיְל / לְקוֹל כִּנּוֹר וְעוּגָבִים מְטִיבִים
אֲשֶׁר רָאָה בְיָדִי כוֹס וְאָמַר / "שְׁתֵה מִבֵּין שְׂפָתַי דַּם עֲנָבִים!"
וְיָרֵחַ כְּמוֹ יוֹד נִכְתְּבָה עַל / כְּסוּת שַׁחַר בְּמֵימֵי הַזְּהָבִים.

שמואל הנגיד

·8·

How exquisite that fawn who woke at night
    To the sound of viol's thrum and tabor's clink,
Who saw the goblet in my hand and said,
    "The grape's blood flows for you between my lips.
        Come, drink."
Behind him stood the moon, a letter C,
    Inscribed on morning's veil in golden ink.

Samuel the Nagid

·8·

No pain in this poem, only voluptuous beauty and pleasure. The words "How exquisite" represent a cliché of the period. The Hebrew words mean literally, "I am ransom for . . . ," meaning, "I would ransom . . . with my life." This expression originated in the tribal customs of pre-Islamic Arabia; in poetry it serves to express admiration for something or someone, or to evoke a lovely memory.

The memory here is of a nighttime revel. It is easy to imagine that the "fawn" of the poem is a young boy or girl servant or entertainer who has dozed off in the course of the evening, while the poet has remained awake, watching him sleep. Perhaps others have fallen asleep, so that only the poet and the musicians are still carrying on the party, as in poem 6. This is the magic moment so often invoked, when the poet, drowsy with drink and surrounded by sleeping friends, is open to special perception and feeling. The youth stirs in his sleep, wakes, and drowsily takes up his role of coquette, extending an erotic invitation.

But this poem is not a love poem, and we hear no more of the flirtation. Love is only a part of the experience described by the poem, not the whole experience. From the fawn's mouth the poet's glance moves upward and outward to seize this experience in its totality, to place the lovely youth and his eroticism in the context of beauty itself. The night sky that frames them both is a black cloth or veil covering the dawn; we know, to our sorrow, that this covering of dawn is only temporary. When it is lifted, the brilliant light of the rising sun will end the party and wash out the poet's magic world.

This world has no need of such garish light. Even the moon does not serve as illumination, but rather as part of the decor, an inscription in golden ink on the black veil, like verses woven onto tapestry or carved into stone. I used the letter "C" in the translation because of its shape, but in Hebrew the letter is *"yod."* [1] Though it is of course possible that the Nagid chose the letter merely because of its shape, it is delightful to seek hidden meaning. Does it stand for *"yayin,"* wine, which has two *yods?* For God, whose name in medieval manuscripts is represented by three or four *yods?* In a rabbinic tradition, God is said to have created this world out of the letter "*he*" and the world to come out of "*yod*."[2] In the neo-Platonic atmosphere prevailing among Jewish thinkers of the Nagid's time, the world to come of the tradition was understood as the equivalent of the Platonic ideal world.[3] Does the use of the letter *yod* here identify the world of the banquet and of beauty with that world of ultimate reality? If so, then the daytime, workaday world that reappears when the veil of dawn is lifted is but a copy of the ideal.

In fact the moon *does* emit light, and against it the poet, the players, the fawn, and the other members of the company seem to stand, at the poem's end, in suspended animation. Perhaps the poet has achieved this effect by creating a situation of intense eroticism that calls for forward motion and resolution, then unexpectedly shifting his attention to the static background, leaving the situation unresolved. Perhaps the effect is unintentional, arising from our modern association of motion against a background of light with the stroboscopic effect. Perhaps it arises from a modern reader's association with Keats' *Ode on a Grecian Urn,* with its poignant evocation of motion and emotion everlastingly unfulfilled. In any case, the scene seems to be photographically frozen, with music, sleepers, and erotic suggestion hanging motionless against a bright night sky, without even a trace of wistfulness in the air.

·9·

```
-- | - ◡ -- | - ◡ -- // | -- | - ◡ -- | - ◡ --
```

הִנֵּה יְמֵי הַקֹּר כְּבָר עָבְרוּ / וִימֵי רְבִיעָה הַסְּתָו קָבְרוּ,
נִרְאוּ בְנֵי הַתּוֹר בְּאַרְצֵנוּ / מֵרֹאשׁ עֲנָפִים זֶה לְזֶה יִקְרוּ.
לָכֵן, מְיֻדָּעִים, בְּרִית רֵעִים / שִׁמְרוּ וְהָאִיצוּ וְאַל תַּמְרוּ!
בּוֹאוּ לְגַנָּתִי וְשׁוֹשַׁנִּים — / רֵיחָם כְּרֵיחַ מָר-דְּרוֹר בְּצָרוּ,
וּשְׁתוּ, עֲלֵי צִצִּים וְקוֹל סִיסִים / לָשִׁיר עֲלֵי טוּב הַזְּמָן חָבְרוּ,
יַיִן כְּדִמְעָתִי עֲלֵי פֵרוּד / רֵעִים וְכִפְנֵי אוֹהֲבִים חָפְרוּ.

שמואל הנגיד

·9·

The days of cold are past and days
    Of spring have buried winter's rains.
The doves are sighted in our land;
    They flock to every lofty bough.
So friends, be true, and keep your word.
    Come quickly, do not disappoint a friend.
But come into my garden. There are
    Roses scented as with myrrh to pluck,
And drink with me, amid the buds and birds
    Assembled there to sing the summer's praise,
Wine, red as my tears for loss
    Of friends, or red as the blush on lovers' cheeks.

Samuel the Nagid

WINE
72

·9·

The tone of this invitation to a garden drinking party turns dark at the end, a common feature of poetry inspired by springtime that we will meet again later in this book. Watching the returning flocks of turtledoves in spring, the poet thinks of his friends and invites them to assemble, like the birds, in his garden. The image carries overtones of well-being, which in Arabic may be expressed by several idioms based on words for assembling.[1]

The friends are to gather with each other and the speaker; they are to unite with elements of nature as well, for in verse 5, the alliterating buds and birds are described as a party already in progress, which the friends are to join. But thoughts of assembly turn to thoughts of dissolution. The color of the wine of spring brings to mind emotions that might seem more appropriate to the rainy season, which verse 1 so decisively declared to be past and buried.

That red wine should make the poet think of tears derives from the conventional poetic imagery, according to which the tears shed by lovers and friends are actually blood flowing up from the heart and out through the eyes. The sight of the birds reminds the poet of his sorrow, for they flock to the garden of their own accord. Friends, too, would flock to the garden, if human life were as orderly as nature. But when friends are separated, by circumstances or by death, they may be summoned as effectively as a flock of birds. Thus the annual reappearance of the birds and other phenomena of spring brings the bitter irony of false comfort. Their reassuring cyclic rhythm reminds us that the individual human life is not cyclic but linear; everything that was once united will eventually be dissolved.

·10·

--|-◡--|-◡-|-◡--

קַח מִצְּבִיָּה דְּמֵי עֵנָב בְּאֶקְדָּחָה
בָּרָה, כְּמוֹ אֵשׁ בְּתוֹךְ בָּרָד מְלֻקָּחָה.
בַּעֲלַת שְׂפָתוֹת כְּחוּט שָׁנִי, וְחֵךְ לָהּ כְּיֵין
הַטּוֹב, וּפִיהָ כְּגוּפָתָהּ מְרֻקָּחָה.
מִדַּם חֲלָלִים קְצֵה יָדָהּ מְאָדָּם — לְכֵן
חֶצְיָהּ כְּאֹדֶם וּמַחֲצִיתָהּ בְּדֹלְחָה!

שמואל הנגיד

·10·

Take from a fawn the crystal filled with blood
    Of grapes, as bright as hailstones filled with fire.
Her lips are a scarlet thread; her kisses, wine;
    Her mouth and body wear the same perfume.
Her hands are crystal wands with ruby tips—
    She tints her fingers with her victim's blood.

Samuel the Nagid

·10·

This poem illustrates well the penchant of Golden Age poets for the startling juxtaposition of opposites. Wine is cold to the taste, but warms the body; it is red but is served in clear or whitish crystal; thus it is a paradoxical combination of fire and ice. These standard images of Arabic poetry happen by a wonderful coincidence to match the description of the plague of hail visited by God upon the Egyptians, as understood by the ancient rabbis: "And there was hail and fire in the midst of the hail," i.e., each hailstone contained fire, but did not melt.[1]

The girl who pours the wine resembles it in color, taste, and fragrance. Thus the hands that pour the wine, with their white skin and henna-dyed tips, match the wine's combination of cold and hot. The color of her fingertips comes not from henna but from the blood of her lovers. Her victims are the revelers themselves, for whom she coquettishly pours. Like the bloody tears of the preceding poem, the bloody fingers of the lady are standard images of love poetry. Touching on the dangerous, even lethal powers of the lovely woman over her admirers, this wine poem serves as a suitable transition to the next chapter, which deals with women and love.

2 Women

For all its charm, the love poetry of the Golden Age can be frustrating to modern readers, for it seems to promise but does not deliver a glimpse into the love life of the great poets of old. We would like to believe that the beautiful women described in the poems were real women, that the passions and heartbreaks really happened. But like the wine poetry to which it is closely related, Hebrew love poetry is conventional in content and stylized in form. Its themes and rhetorical figures are drawn from the common fund of literary material that the Jewish literati first acquired through their education in Arabic poetry, then used and recycled. Much of this material was collected and classified in 1027 by ʿAli Ibn Ḥazm, a distinguished Muslim theologian and contemporary of Samuel the Nagid, in a delightful book entitled *The Dove's Neck Ring*, which has been translated into English.[1]

The stylization that prevails in the genre does not rule out the possibility that individual poems may have arisen out of real love affairs. Arabic literature knew the conception of the great passion. Sometimes it pushed this conception to the point of absurdity, as in countless anecdotes of people who died for love. However, many stories, particularly in *The Dove's Neck Ring*, bear an air of reality fostered by their attributing a variety of feelings and gradations of attachment to the lovers.

But the individuality of these stories is absent from both the Arabic and Hebrew poetry. Even the celebrated love affair of the renowned Arabic poet Ibn Zaidun and the princess Wallada, about which we are reliably and minutely informed by prose sources, is wanly depicted in the lovers' own poetry; Ibn Zaidun's most brilliant poem to Wallada contains much that is routine in its fifty long verses.[2] The same is true of the love poetry of al-Muʿtamid, the prince of Seville, to his wife, the former slave Iʿtimad.[3]

We should not blame the poets for our frustration at not finding in their poetry the hard biographical data we seek; their purpose was to write poetry, not autobiography. The same vagueness about facts obscures the identity of the beloved subject of Shakespeare's sonnets, to take only one case out of many in Western literature. But although Shakespeare's sonnets lack intelligible references to concrete biographical data and use many conventional elements of form and theme, their distinctive individuality within Elizabethan love poetry is rare in medieval Arabic and Hebrew poetry. Allowances must be made for the fact that even sophisticated Western readers are not attuned to the nuances of medieval Arabic and Hebrew rhetoric. Efforts by sympathetic Western scholars are beginning to expose the subtleties of this literature and to provide tools for an appreciation of the poets' craft and a more discriminating evaluation of their achievement.[4] But even taking this reservation into account, we are left with a very large body of poetry that is content with a limited repertoire of familiar themes and images. We must acknowledge that medieval lovers of poetry, both Arabs and Jews, simply enjoyed the repetition.

We must accept the fact that the love celebrated in the poetry, even when based on actual experience, is not given poetic form for the sake of individual expression but on behalf of a communal ideal. It is this ideal, the celebration of a life devoted to joy and beauty, that is the nexus between the poetry of love and the poetry of wine. Before addressing the particular aspects of the ideal that inform the love poetry, we must realize that the poetry's conventionality does not argue against its sincerity. Feelings are real whether they arise from real love or imaginary love. We must remember that the relationship celebrated by the poem is not that of lover and beloved but of observer and beauty observed.

The relationship depicted in secular love poetry becomes clearer through its religious analogue, the relationship of cantor and God in the poetry of the synagogue. In this ocean of Hebrew poetry, composed over more than a millennium in nearly every Jewish community in Europe and the Middle East, we find variations on a body of themes and images set forth in verse forms only slightly less rigid and limited than those of Arabic verse. Yet this stylized literature was avidly cultivated by pious Jews and eagerly attended to by worshippers, serving for centuries as a beloved form of expression for communal religious values and feelings. No matter how much we are disappointed by its uniformity, we cannot help being impressed and even moved by its sincerity.[5]

As with wine poems, it is necessary to distinguish love poetry proper from other types of poems that incorporate its themes and motifs.

The *qaṣida* poem, described in the introduction to Chapter I, frequently begins like a love poem, evoking memories of old love affairs, describing a beautiful woman, or making other use of elements of love poetry. Such openings, called *nasīb,* were standard in the pre-Islamic *qaṣida,* where they were usually part of a complex of conventional introductory themes leading up to the poem's real subject. We have seen that a wine poem sometimes serves as the opening of a Hebrew *qaṣida,* but for this purpose amatory poems are more commonly used. One reason for their predominance is the simple force of tradition, the erotic *nasīb* having the prestige of antiquity. But the inner reason is that the classic theme of the *qaṣida* is friendship or admiration for an individual, an emotion closely related to love and often expressed in the same terms. For example, the essential themes of the separation of lovers and the nostalgic evocation of past joy create an appropriately elegiac atmosphere in which the poet can lament his separation from the friend or patron to whom the poem is addressed. Furthermore, it is not uncommon for the poet to portray the friend or patron in imagery similar to that used for lovers. As in the case of the wine poem, this anthology avoids the *qaṣida* in favor of lighter, more unified poems. For the same reason it avoids panegyrical *muwash-shaḥāt*, even though there are many fine examples of such poems beginning with amatory preludes and making a transition to panegyric in the manner of the *qaṣida*.

It is very important to distinguish true love poems from wedding poems, much as these genres may resemble each other. Epithalamia may make use of the erotic images of secular love poetry to a surprising extent, given the solemnity and religious character of the circumstances they celebrate. Yet they are in spirit a type of panegyric, in which the subject is the couple or their families. Furthermore, in the epithalamium the poet is not a party to the relationship but a spokesman for the community celebrating the union. In this capacity his function resembles more that of the liturgical than the love poet. The community celebrating a marriage is different from the community observing a love affair, even if it is composed partly of the same individuals, and the differing attitudes of these two communities toward love produce significant differences in the poetry, even when they exploit the same poetic resources. Accordingly, wedding poems have also been excluded from this anthology.

The typical medieval Hebrew love poem belongs to a genre known in the Arabic literary tradition as *ghazal,* resembling in form the wine poems.[6] They are short, usually four to six verses, and are composed in the classical prosodic patterns of quantitative meter and monorhyme borrowed from Arabic.[7] Besides these short poems, there exists a rather large body of *muwashshaḥāt* devoted exclusively to love; indeed, the entire genre seems originally to have been composed exclusively of love poetry, the panegyrical *muwashshah* being a secondary development. Several *muwashshaḥāt* that are truly about love are included to represent a variety of love poetry of distinctive character and outstanding importance. Since they draw their themes, diction, and rhetoric from the same sources as poems of the *ghazal* type, their importance resides entirely in their forms of versification, which make them attractive to Western ears.

Most love poems fall into two categories, resembling the division of the wine poem into descriptive and meditative types. They may be designated *descriptive* love poems and *petitionary* love poems.[8]

Descriptive love poems closely resemble descriptive wine poems in that they select certain elements of the object to be described and attach to them comparisons and figures of speech drawn from the traditional fund; the main difference is that in love poetry the object is a living person instead of an inanimate thing, and even this difference is not so great as it might at first appear. In petitionary love poems, the poet implores the beloved to pay attention to him, return his affection, renew an earlier tie now broken, or the like. The essential difference between the two types is that the petitionary poem poses as an instrument of the love affair itself, representing a real or imaginary moment in life, from which it derives a dynamic character; the descriptive poems are static and do not point to a particular circumstance as the point of origin. The typical petitionary poem is addressed directly to the beloved in the second person (though it may be couched in the form of a prayer, with God in the second person and the beloved in the third, or as a meditation within the poet himself in the second person); whereas the descriptive poem is typically addressed to someone else, referring to the beloved in the third person. This analysis is schematic, for the two categories may overlap in a single poem; but since the poems are short their primary mode is usually unambiguous.

Descriptive love poems concentrate on the beloved's body. The parts usually treated are, in descending order: the hair, eyebrows, cheeks, mouth, throat, breasts, belly, waist, and thighs; but these are not described in a way that would identify them as belonging to any particular person, and qualitatively distinctive traits are never mentioned. The descriptions consist simply of familiar figures of speech; the eyebrows are shaped like bows; the eyes shoot arrows that wound or kill the lover; the cheeks are rouged with the lover's blood; and so forth. The beloved's superiority to all others is through degree, not kind; she possesses no quality that would render her unique except the highest degree of those characteristics expected in a beloved.

She does not even possess a name. It is sometimes said that the love poets' practice of referring to the beloved by such stock pet names as "fawn" or "gazelle" arose out of the need to protect the beloved from exposure; thus these epithets would resemble in function the *senhals* of the troubadours.[9] Whether or not this historical explanation is correct, it is far less important than the perfect aptness of this form of address for a genre that habitually presents the beloved as a type rather than an individual. This approach to love is diametrically opposed to the current popular ideology, which stresses individuality, and in which "special" is a code word admiringly applied to both persons and relationships. In the present translations I have generally rendered all these code words as "fawn," whether they actually mean fawn, gazelle, mountain goat, deer, buck, or doe, in the hope of establishing in this anthology an association between the standard image of the beloved and the one regularly repeating term.

The lack of individuality in the beloved has another ramification that is even less familiar, and decidedly less comfortable, to Western readers; that is its unclear gender. It is a peculiarity of Arabic and Hebrew love poetry that the beloved is regularly, though not consistently, referred to in the masculine gender. Unfortunately, in the minds of most present-day Western readers, love poetry by a man addressed to a (grammatically) masculine beloved triggers such powerful attitudes about homosexuality as to block the way to a calm literary and cultural appraisal of the poetry. Official Judaism has always viewed homosexuality with loathing. The horror aroused by the topic has led to angry exchanges between scholars and frantic exegetical efforts to protect the honor of the medieval poets. So much attention has been focused on the purely historical question of whether the poets actually practiced homosexuality that little has been left over for more relevant questions. What does this kind of poetry tell us about the concept of love held by the Andalusian courtier-rabbis? How did this particular type of poetry satisfy for them the universal drive to find artistic expression for important feelings? This larger topic will be addressed toward the end of this introduction; for now it is enough to place the homosexuality of the poetry in its theoretical context, among the many features of descriptive love poetry, including the use of conventional rhetorical figures instead of true description and stock epithets instead of names, that tend to reduce the beloved to a type. The use of the masculine gender creates an atmosphere not of maleness but of indefinite sexuality. The beloved is a type: not a type of female beauty so familiar to our culture, nor yet a type of male beauty such as one would expect in a truly homosexual culture, but a type of beauty itself, an individual embodiment of an ideal to which it points the way. Sex, in its strict sense meaning the *division* between the two human forms of beauty, is not only irrelevant but also actually leads *away* from the central theme of universal ideal beauty. To be true to the point of view of the poets themselves, we should probably speak not of *reducing* the beloved from an individual to a type but rather of elevating her.[10]

To return to the descriptive love poetry: The morality, intelligence, and spiritual life of the beloved are completely outside the scope of this literature. Her character is of interest only in relation to the lover, and the most striking feature in the standard description is her unmitigated hard-heartedness. Never is she described as being in love or even capable of love, but only of arousing love in the hearts of her admirers. The ability to be moved is not part of the standard image of the beloved. This frigidity is represented on the rhetorical level by comparison of parts of the beloved's body to precious metals or stones, which are desirable, beautiful, and inviting, but cold to the touch. Comparison of her face to the sun suggests not inner warmth, but a remoteness concomitant with transcendent beauty, and the power to arouse feelings in ordinary mortals—just as the distant sun stimulates the earth to fecundity without itself being affected.

It should be clear by now that the genre we have called "descriptive love poetry" is not really about love; it is actually descriptive poetry of the same kind as was discussed in the introduction to Chapter I. It is not hard to imagine that much of it even originated at wine parties, where the *sáki* would naturally become the subject of poetic improvisations just like any other available object. The flirtatiousness with which the *sáki* performed his office and the deliberate sexual ambiguity of his costume have already been mentioned. The *sáki* was trained to use his beauty and wit to arouse the revelers and frustrate them at the same time. It may well have been the "look but don't touch" aspect of his function that created the image of the cold beauty in descriptive love poetry. Moses Ibn Ezra, describing a wine party in the introduction to one of his great *qaṣidas*, says:

> The *sáki* has a weakling's lisp, and yet
> Brave soldiers fall before the words he speaks.

His eyes are widened not with paint, but charm;
　　Abundant loveliness they have, and magic power.
Sometimes they deal out life and sometimes death
　　According as their glance is firm or weak.
They show the path of chasteness to the pure;
　　To wicked men they teach the lecher's way.
. . . .
With our imaginary mouths we kiss his lips;
　　With eyes alone we pluck his beauty's buds;
We sate our eyes on his abundant grace;
　　Our lips the while are faint with famine's pangs.[11]

Many such passages confirm the link between the genre of de-
scriptive love poetry and the wine party, though there is no reason
to think that the wine party actually created the genre.

The petitionary love poem, even when it makes extensive use
of descriptive motifs, essentially concerns not the beloved but the
relationship; indeed, since the relationship is either finished or
imaginary, and the inner life of the beloved is never described, the
poem really deals with the lover's feelings about the beloved. The
strictly external description of the beloved contrasts with the inter-
nal image of the lover. We learn nothing about his character, life, or
activities, except in relation to her; the only action attributed to
him is the addressing of the poem to her. He speaks of himself only
as a bearer of emotions; and the emotions which he expresses
openly or which may be inferred from his supplications are largely
the negative ones of passivity, humiliation, suffering, and unful-
filled longing. Her very beauty frightens him. Her earlocks are
snakes that would bite him if he dared caress her cheeks, and her
breasts are lances to transfix anyone who dares embrace her. Her
beauty reduces him to abjectness, while her intransigence fills him
with self-pity and, occasionally, anger. His mood is generally som-
ber. His love is a disease, a destructive obsession isolating him from
the rest of society. The passion that he feels has never been experi-
enced by another lover and cannot be understood by his friends. As
his beloved is unique in her beauty, so is he in the extremity of his
devotion.

Thus to the celebration of beauty in the descriptive love poems
and the other minor descriptive genres, the petitionary poetry adds
an important new element: the sensitivity of the man who is af-

fected by this beauty. For when love poetry strays from the rhetorical decoration of the beautiful lady or boy, it strays to one subject alone: the emotions of the poet-lover. As a lover, he speaks of his suffering to demonstrate to the beloved his worthiness; but as a poet he is also addressing an audience, displaying a sensitivity so extreme as to weaken his body and undermine his morale, as if to say, "Such is my capacity for submission to the power of beauty."

The love poet's display of himself as isolated from his fellow man and unable to satisfy his longing for happiness has its parallel in some of the wine poems. Although the drinking takes place in a group, and the poet speaks with pleasure of enjoying wine in the company of his friends, we have already seen him lying awake after the other revelers have dozed off; and we shall be hearing some of the musings of the lonely drinker in Chapter III. Without going into detail right now about the contents of his reverie, we can see in poems 6, 7, and 9 the wine poet's sense of himself as belonging to a small, inner circle of individuals who are truly sensitive to the beauty and joy around them. The price of his sensitivity is frustration and loneliness.

The reader of medieval Hebrew love poetry is continually confronted with the paradox of poets staking a claim to uniqueness for themselves and their beloveds by means of a great stock of clichés; thus the style of their work is at odds with one of its dominant themes. The only way to resolve this paradox is to fight down our own desire for heroic lovers in the Western mold, and to acknowledge that the courtier-rabbis of the Golden Age used poetry to a large extent as a ritual expression of an ideal shared by their social class. Highly self-conscious, fiercely proud of their unique position vis-à-vis the contemporary Jewish masses and past Jewish leadership, they used poetry to articulate their devotion to beauty as a cardinal value of the spiritual life. The poet's audience never tired of his celebration of beauty and of himself as a uniquely sensitive man, just as the individual members of the community never tired of the stereotyped panegyrics addressed to them by their literary protégés. The poet's sensitivity was their own, and in his longing they found themselves. Hence the object of the love poet's adoration is left unidentified, and the description is as unspecific as possible. She is not an individual but a shared experience. The stylization of the language and imagery used to articulate that experience is calculated to include the audience.

Examining more closely the character of that experience, we find that it is not primarily an experience of love, the consciousness of a passionate union between two souls, but a deeply felt admiration for an object which may itself remain unmoved; it is an esthetic rather than a loving experience. The uniquely sensitive lover of the petitionary poetry is frustrated by the impossibility of crossing the boundary between these types of experience. By expressing his frustration he displays the intensity of his feelings. Because his beloved is a person, who ought to be subject to human emotions, the frustration caused by her remaining unmoved is the more poignant. In this poignancy lies the special appeal of love poetry over the other minor genres, which celebrate the beauty of inanimate objects.

What is the historical reality behind the poems? Did the courtier-rabbis really have flirtations and even love affairs? We will not be able to discuss this question productively unless we rid ourselves of the monolithic view of Jewish sexuality and investigate the source material. I do not know of a single prose anecdote of a love affair involving a member of the circle of Jewish poets that would provide documentary confirmation of the kind of love life portrayed in the poetry. And yet the same reasoning that led us to affirm the participation of Jews in wine parties would lead us to affirm cautiously their participation in the kind of love life fashionable in their milieu. We have seen that Arabic wine poetry did not exist in isolation, but was part of a social institution that flourished in defiance of official Islamic law and sentiment, attracting adherents even among the political and religious leadership of the Muslim majority. The same was true of love, for despite the aversion of religious leaders to sexual promiscuity and homosexuality, both were practiced widely and even celebrated in poetry by prominent Muslim figures. What justification is there for assuming that the Hebrew poetry describing exactly the same social institutions does not reflect the same reality, and the same dichotomized way of life? [12] Even if the Hebrew poetry could be proved a mere aping of literary conventions, we would still be left to account for the poets' devoting so much intellectual energy and creative power to these particular conventions, so removed from those of traditional Judaism. The intellectual problem does not disappear even if we assume that the poets were merely fantasizing; for the fact remains that in the minds of the religious and intellectual leadership of Andalusian Jewry, two different ideals coexisted. That is exactly what makes them so interesting.[13]

The questions raised by the homosexual love poetry are not essentially different from those raised by Hebrew love poetry in general. Here at least a few anecdotes and legal responsa provide some documentation from outside the world of imaginative literature.[14] But these data do not shed light on the meaning of the poetry. They only confirm that individual cases of homosexual behavior occurred, which we might have guessed, and that official Judaism did not approve, which we have always known.

It is necessary to state clearly that there *is* a homosexual element in the love poetry, for some readers have attempted to deny even this.[15] One example, possibly the first of its kind in Hebrew, should be conclusive. It is the work of Isaac Ibn Mar Saul of the late tenth to early eleventh centuries, who also wrote a delicate penitential poem still widely recited by pious Jews.

> Delightful Spanish fawn,
>   Work of mighty God,
> Who gave him power to rule
>   Every living thing.
> Face like the lovely moon,
>   Atop a handsome form;
> Locks of royal blue
>   Against a brow of pearl;
> Joseph-like his face;
>   Hair like Absalom;
> Handsome as David he;
>   Me, like Uriah, he kills.
> . . . . [16]

As Schirmann pointed out, the comparison of the fawn with biblical men renowned for their beauty rules out the possibility that the poet is speaking of a woman in the masculine gender, which sometimes does occur. That the object of desire in the poetry is often male is as certain as any point in a medieval Hebrew poem can be. We might be tempted to explain away the homosexuality of some of the love poetry by assuming that the persona of the speaker is female, as in the Portuguese *cantigas de amigo*[17]; but the comparison of the speaker to Uriah the Hittite in the last line quoted might almost have been devised specifically to block this route of escape. We must acknowledge that in at least some of the love poems, both personae are male.

That it has been at all possible to deny the existence of homosexual love in medieval Hebrew poetry is attributable to the surprising fact that the thousands of lines of descriptive love poetry contain very few specific details that unambiguously denote maleness in the beloved. The main indicators of gender are grammatically masculine nouns and verbs and comparisons to male heroes of old. The only male characteristic ever mentioned seems to be the down on the youth's cheek.[18] This reticence about sexual details is not a result of shyness about homosexuality, but characterizes the poetry as a whole. Even poems addressed to or praising women usually identify the beloved as female only by means of grammatical gender, not by reference to physical traits.

Although the experience of sexual love is never far from the poet's mind, neither the sex of the beloved nor the physical act itself ever received much stress. This genre manages to be sensual without being sexual. It might seem salacious against the background of traditional Jewish literature, but in the world of Abu Nuwas and Ibn Quzman, it is chasteness itself.

Hebrew love poetry is no more about debauchery than Hebrew wine poetry is about drunken binges. There may have been medieval Jews who engaged in both, just as there were medieval Jews—probably the great majority—who never attended a wine party nor heard a Hebrew love poem; but the poetry tells us next to nothing about these extremes. There are scattered hints of uncourtly, blameworthy love, or at least of blameworthy women.[19] Probably that is the meaning of the contrast between "fawns of the field" and "fawns of the palace" encountered here and there in the poetry, as, for example, in the speech of one of the women in the love story of Ibn Ṣaqbel:

> I am a mountain-goat of the indoors, a doe of the courts. Never have I lived in forests nor have I known the cloven mountains. I am a palace woman brought up in dignity.[20]

But the aristocratic character of medieval Hebrew poetry virtually precludes the possibility of our learning from it about Jewish Bohemian life.

Courtly Hebrew love poetry, like courtly Arabic love poetry, deals not with sex but with beauty. Its great innovation was not the introduction of homosexuality into its thematic repertoire, but the spiritualization of love itself, a truly Greek notion fundamentally at odds with both biblical and rabbinic thinking. Love, whether consummated or chaste, whether heterosexual or homosexual, is spiritual when it is understood by its practitioners as the ennobling service of beauty itself; when its sensual pleasures point the way upward, rather than toward the earthbound extremes of licentiousness on the one hand, domesticity and procreation on the other.[21] Within this great innovation, the quiet use of the masculine gender in love poetry takes its place as a variation on a truly great theme. W. H. Auden in his introduction to Shakespeare's sonnets remarks that

> . . . men and women whose sexual tastes are perfectly normal, but who enjoy and understand poetry, have always been able to read them as expressions of what they understand by the word *love*, without finding the masculine pronoun an obstacle.[22]

This certainly applies to the poems we are about to read.

$$-\cup-|-|-\cup-$$

דַּדֵּי יְפַת תֹּאַר לֵיל חֲבֹק
וּשְׂפַת יְפַת מַרְאֶה יוֹמָם נְשֹׁק!

וּגְעַר בְּכָל מֵרִיב, יוֹעֵץ לְפִי
דַרְכּוֹ, וְקַח יֹשֶׁר נִמְצָא בְּפִי:
אֵין הַחַיּוֹת רַק עִם יַלְדֵי יָפִי,
כִּי גֻנְּבוּ מֵעֵדֶן לַעֲשֹׁק
חַיִּים — וְאֵין אִישׁ חַי לֹא יַחֲשֹׁק!

נַסֵּךְ לְבָבְךָ בְּשִׂמְחוֹת וְשִׂישׂ
וּשְׁתֵה עֲלֵי יֵבֶל נֵבֶל עָסִיס
יַיִן, לְקוֹל נֵבֶל עִם תּוֹר וְסִיס,

וּרְקֹד וְגִיל, גַּם כַּף עַל כַּף סְפֹק,
וּשְׁכַר וְדֵלֶת יַעֲלַת חֵן דְּפֹק.

זֶה הוּא נְעִים תֵּבֵל — קַח חֶלְקְךָ
מֶנּוּ כְּאִיל מִלּוּאִים, חָקְךָ
שִׂימָה מְנָת רָאשֵׁי עַם צִדְקְךָ:
אַל תֶּחֱשֶׂה לִמְצֹץ שָׂפָה וְרֹק,
עַד תֶּאֱחֹז חָקְךָ — חָזֶה וְשׁוֹק!

משה אבן עזרא

·11·

Caress a lovely woman's breast by night,
And kiss some beauty's lips by morning light.

    Silence those who criticize you, those
    Officious talkers. Take advice from me:
  With beauty's children only can we live.
Kidnapped were they from Paradise to gall
The living; living men are lovers all.

    Immerse your heart in pleasure and in joy,
    And by the bank a bottle drink of wine,
    Enjoy the swallow's chirp and viol's whine.
Laugh, dance, and stamp your feet upon the floor!
Get drunk, and knock at dawn on some girl's door.

    This is the joy of life, so take your due.
    You too deserve a portion of the Ram
    Of Consecration, like your people's chiefs.
To suck the juice of lips do not be shy,
But take what's rightly yours—the breast and thigh!

Moses Ibn Ezra

·11·

Since Moses Ibn Ezra wrote a treatise on the theory of poetry and another theoretical treatise on figurative language, it seems in character that he should have devoted a poem or two to the theory of the good life.[1] Similar in tone to the sermonic wine poems of the preceding chapter but far more extreme, this poem may be the most forceful recommendation of the life of pleasure bequeathed to us by the Golden Age. It seems to adumbrate a whole theory of pleasure. It is a poem touched by philosophy.

Unfortunately, it seems to be only partly preserved. *Muwash-shaḥāt* such as this one almost always have five stanzas; it may be that at some point in the course of transmission two stanzas offended a traditionally pious copyist.[2] Such censorship is easy to imagine, for some of the extant lines come dangerously close to blasphemy.

The key to the poet's thinking is in the first stanza: "With beauty's children only can we live. / Kidnapped were they from Paradise to gall / The living; living men are lovers all." "Paradise" in the translation stands for "Eden" in the Hebrew, the garden of delight where God originally intended man to live; the word itself means "luxury," "dainty," or "delight." The expression "beauty's children" is literally "beauty's daughters," a very common type of Arabic idiom designating possessors of a given characteristic, such as "brothers of wisdom" meaning "the wise"; or individual members of a class, such as "daughters of fate," meaning "days" or "vicissitudes."[3] The expression could mean simply "beautiful girls," as glossed by Brody, were it not for the astonishing and perhaps unique use to which it is put in these lines, which tersely propound a mythical way of thinking about man's relationship to love and beauty.

Beauty is embodied in individuals, here called "Beauty's children," who have been abducted from Paradise, the source of all mankind. Understanding Paradise as the biblical Garden of Eden, we thus have a whimsical explanation for the susceptibility of mankind to beauty and to love. But if Paradise is understood to mean the Platonic ideal world, then the creatures who arouse us to love, the children of Beauty, are individual representatives of the

Beautiful. No wonder all mankind is susceptible to them; in the neo-Platonic world view current in Moses Ibn Ezra's time, all individual things yearn to return to their point of origin, the universal from which they emanated. This universal, ideal world is called *maqor* in Hebrew, or "source," as in Ibn Gabirol's neo-Platonic treatise entitled "The Source of Life."[4] In this image, the world of universals is ordinarily thought of as a well, from which flow the particulars; the "source" is also sometimes thought of as a mine, designated in Arabic by the word *ma'dan*. How the medieval Hebrew intellectuals must have delighted in this word, whose root is *'dn*, the same as the Hebrew word for Eden! The word itself must have seemed to confirm the Platonic allegorization of the biblical story of Paradise, of which dim echoes have survived.[5]

The poet does not dwell on the abduction of Beauty's daughters. We would like to think that he has in mind a specific myth known to his audience, but this is not necessary. "Kidnapped" need mean no more than that Beauty's daughters are not at home in this world, and that like the soul they yearn to be restored to their source. We do not know whether neo-Platonists of Moses Ibn Ezra's time had more elaborate myths; but the yearning of the soul to leave the body and return to its source is a commonplace of neo-Platonic spirituality.

While Beauty's children are in the material world they have an automatic and universal effect. We cannot help responding to the Beauty whose shadow they are; though captives in the material world, they captivate their captors. This idea is reinforced by a pun so common in Hebrew love poetry that it would not deserve mention except for the use to which it is put. *'Ashaq* rhymes at the end of the first stanza with *ḥashaq*, "to oppress" with "to love."[6] The rhyme implies that our susceptibility to love results from our experiencing in it a superior power.

Though the words here translated as "lovely woman" may mean no more than that, in talmudic law the Hebrew phrase is also a technical term deriving from the Bible, where it denotes a female war captive taken as a wife by an Israelite warrior.[7] The military origin of the phrase has no bearing on the poem, but the connotation of a non-Jewish woman as the object of desire affects its message. The poem sets up beauty as a rule of life; the implicit message of the term *"yefat toar"* is that the community of beauty's devotees is not limited to national groups such as Mozarabic, Arab, Berber, or Jewish, but comprises an international class. Thus mankind is endowed from its origin with beauty and the capacity to be affected by beauty. Unreasonable people like the "watchers" of poem 6 pretend this is not so, but they must be resisted; for there is no real life without beauty and love.

The second stanza itemizes pleasures we have come to know from the wine poetry, accompanied by standard puns and sound plays, which I have tried to suggest by means of alliterations in the English version.[8] These delights all take place out of doors, the idyllic setting of the wine poem that is the poet's approximation to Eden. The only suggestion of an indoor activity is the mention of a "girl's door" at the end of the stanza, but this is a figurative expression, derived from the image of a beggar, and here meaning "to pay court." It was probably selected because of several biblical passages that associate doors with sexual activity.[9] The dalliance does not necessarily take place indoors.

Indoors or out, the intention is frankly sexual, as the final stanza makes clear. What is shocking about these lines is not so much the explicit reference to sexuality as the almost midrashic association of sexual pleasure with the Ram of Consecration. This sacrifice was offered as part of the ceremony through which Aaron and his sons were consecrated as priests. Because of special rituals involving its breast and right thigh, the phrase "breast of the wave-offering and thigh of the heave-offering" recur with refrain-like regularity in the biblical chapters describing the ceremony.[10] Moses Ibn Ezra may not have been the first to make jocular use of this phrase in connection with sexual behavior and was definitely not the last to do so; but he may be the only one to use the phrase as more than a joke, by alluding to the context from which it is taken. He has transformed the biblical account of the consecration of priests into a secular fantasy of induction into a radically different elite. The "breast and thigh" of the poem are not the portion of the biblical priests, but rather of "your people's chiefs"—the courtier class, the privileged devotees of beauty, of which Ibn Ezra was a most articulate member.

‎-- -- ‎◡ -- ‎◡ --

‎תַּאֲוַת לְבָבִי וּמַחְמַד עֵינִי —
‎עֹפֶר לְצִדִּי וְכוֹס בִּימִינִי!

‎רַבּוּ מְרִיבַי — וְלֹא אֶשְׁמָעֵם,
‎בּוֹא, הַצְּבִי, וַאֲנִי אַכְנִיעֵם,
‎וּזְמָן יְכַלֵּם וּמָוֶת יִרְעֵם.
‎בּוֹא, הַצְּבִי, קוּם וְהַבְרִיאֵנִי
‎מִצּוּף שְׂפָתְךָ וְהַשְׂבִּיעֵנִי!

‎לָמָּה יְנִיאוּן לְבָבִי, לָמָּה?
‎אִם בַּעֲבוּר חֵטְא וּבִגְלַל אַשְׁמָה
‎אֶשְׁגֶּה בְיָפְיֵךְ — אֲדֹנָי שָׁמָּה!
‎אַל יֵט לְבָבְךָ בְּנִיב מְעַנֶּיךָ,
‎אִישׁ מַעֲקַשִׁים, וּבוֹא נַסֵּנִי.

‎נִפְתָּה, וַקַּמְנוּ אֱלֵי בֵית אִמּוֹ,
‎וַיֵּט לְעֹל סֻבֳּלֵי אֶת שִׁכְמוֹ,
‎לַיְלָה וְיוֹמָם אֲנִי רַק עִמּוֹ.
‎אֶפְשֹׁט בְּגָדָיו — וְיַפְשִׁיטֵנִי,
‎אִינַק שְׂפָתָיו — וְיֵינִיקֵנִי.

‎כַּאֲשֶׁר לְבָבִי בְּעֵינָיו נִפְקַד,
‎גַּם עַל פְּשָׁעַי בְּיָדוֹ נִשְׁקָד —
‎דָּרַשׁ תְּנוּאוֹת וְאַפּוֹ פָקַד,
‎צָעַק בְּאַף "רַב לְךָ, עָזְבֵנִי,
‎אַל תֶּהְדְּפֵנִי וְאַל תַּתְעֵנִי!"

‎אַל תֶּאֱנַף בִּי, צְבִי, עַד כַּלֵּה,
‎הַפְלֵא רְצוֹנְךָ, יְדִידִי, הַפְלֵא,
‎וּנְשַׁק יְדִידְךָ וְחֶפְצוֹ מַלֵּא!
‎אִם יֵשׁ בְּנַפְשְׁךָ חַיּוֹת — חַיֵּנִי,
‎אוֹ חֶפְצְךָ לַהֲרֹג — הָרְגֵנִי!

‎משה אבן עזרא

·12·

The joy of my eyes and my heart's delight—
A fawn at my left and a cup in my right!

    Many men fault me, but I don't mind.
    Come, watch me crush them, beautiful hind.
    Old age consume them! Death to their kind!
Come, my gazelle, give me something to eat;
The mead of your lips makes our banquet complete.

    Why do they want to discourage me, why?
    What in the world is the sin if I
    Thrill to your beauty? There's Adonai!
Pay them no heed, and in their despite,
Come and caress me, stubborn wight.

    He listened, and let me come home with him.
    He did what I wanted, obeyed every whim.
    By day and by night we dallied within.
I took off his clothes and he took off mine,
He offered his lips and I drank of their wine.

    Just when my heart was no longer free,
    Just then he started to find fault with me.
    He quarreled and spoke to me angrily,
"Get along with you, and be on your way!
Don't you seduce me and lead me astray!"

    Don't be so angry with me, gazelle.
    Think of me kindly, and love me well.
    Give me a kiss, and do not rebel.
You can bestow on me life, if you will,
Or use the power of your beauty to kill.

Moses Ibn Ezra

Though it turns on a lovers' quarrel that remains unresolved at the end, this poem is not weighted down by the tone of self-pity so characteristic of Hebrew and Arabic love poetry. The opening couplet, which, as explained in the introduction, probably served as a refrain, reminds us that as far as the poet is concerned, any love will do. In the following stanzas he describes his lust for the particular "gazelle" who is directly addressed at the poem's end; but any effect of seriousness is cancelled out by the recurrences of the refrain. The particular fawn at his left hand matters no more than the particular cup in his right hand. The lightness of the sentiment matches the rollicking meter.

The "blamers" who wish to discourage the poet are the same proponents of conventional morality who had dozed off in poem 6. In love poetry, the lover has two types of opponent: the protectors of the beloved, who are dangerous, and his own well-meaning friends, who are nuisances, continually harping on the impropriety and dangerousness of his conduct. For the poet they are a useful nuisance, providing an ethos of prudence as background against which he can display the extremity of his feelings or his heroic recklessness.[1]

Though this poem makes no reference to Eden or other gardens, it does make symbolic use of the idea of significant space. Even before naming the actual site of the tryst in the third stanza, the idea is prepared by the words "There's *Adonai*" in stanza 2. This use of one of the names of God is astonishing in a secular context. Although the word *Adonai,* meaning "my Lord," was originally used to avoid using God's proper name, *Yahweh,* it had long since acquired some of the numinousness of the ineffable name itself. It was never written and was pronounced only in formal, rabbinically authorized circumstances.[2] Yet here it is used for the purpose of justifying the poet's infatuation with his fawn, in a metrical context that rules out the possibility that some other word was substituted during recitation.

To understand the poet's meaning it is necessary to know that the expression "There's *Adonai*" is a quotation from the Bible. It is the conclusion of the book of Ezekiel, the summary of nine chapters describing the Prophet's vision of Jerusalem rebuilt in the Messianic Era: "The name of the city from that day on shall be 'The Lord is There.'"[3] Through this verse the fawn of the poem is associated with a dazzling vision of the heavenly city, not yet revealed to mankind at large, but a reality nevertheless. Like Eden in the preceding poem, this image must be understood in a neo-Platonic context. The world of the fawn exists at a higher level of reality than that of mankind at large; the poet's detractors can neither understand nor appreciate his yearning, for their world is one of unreality and delusion.

This interpretation is bolstered by the phrase "Let me come home with him," which, literally translated, reads, "We rose [and went] to his mother's house." These words derive from the Song of Songs and were understood by the traditional rabbinic exegesis to refer allegorically to the Temple.[4] The conception that a Temple exists in heaven parallel to the Temple in Jerusalem was developed in detail by the Midrash.[5] This ancient vision may or may not have derived from the Platonic concept of an ideal world; certainly it provided a foundation for an allegorical exegesis of all biblical references to the Temple when Jewish intellectuals in the Arab world came under the sway of neo-Platonism. This may seem a heavy burden for such an unassuming sentence as "We rose [and went] to his mother's house"; but in the highly conventional world of medieval Hebrew love poetry the verse cries out for attention because it is not part of the standard repertoire of images used by love poets, nor does it reflect any conceivable social reality. Unless the words are interpreted along the lines suggested here, they are empty. In summary, the poem's two allusions to the Temple, like the allusion to Eden in the preceding poem, suggest an ideal world of beauty, of which the fawn is a particular representative.

Despite the intricacy of this exposition, the poem is not a philosophical treatise but a frivolous piece that uses philosophical ideas current and readily accessible to educated men. It concerns an attempted but unsuccessful seduction; the speaker's philosophy of love is part of his "line," and comes close to achieving his purpose. The fawn, however, is willing to go only so far. After leading the poet-lover on, the fawn assails him with reproaches. The tone, of course, is tongue-in-cheek. The suitor's intentions are never in doubt; by the third stanza the dalliance has already advanced far beyond the mere intellectual contemplation of celestial beauty. But capriciousness is part of the stock character of the fawn, and nothing in the lover's philosophical seduction-speech implies that he would be satisfied with less than full consummation. His philosophy is intended to justify the poet's sexual intentions, not to obscure them.[6]

‎— — — ‎ ‿ ‎— — —

‎סוֹד לִבִּי וּמַצְפּוּנִי
‎גִּלּוּ נַחֲלֵי עֵינִי.

‎מָרִיב, הַחֲשֵׁה הֶרֶף!
‎צְבִי לָמַד טְרֹף טֶרֶף
‎עַז פָּנִים קָשֶׁה עֹרֶף,
‎חִשְׁקוֹ הֶעֱצִיבַנִי
‎וּבְלִי לֵב עֲזַבַנִי.

‎עֹפֶר דָּלְלוּ מָתְנָיו,
‎שֶׁמֶשׁ רַד לְמוּל פָּנָיו,
‎וּבְחִצֵּי שְׁתֵּי עֵינָיו
‎אֶת נוּמִי גְזָלַנִי
‎וּבְכָל פֶּה אֲכָלַנִי.

‎לֹא אֶשְׁכַּח יְמֵי חֶלְדִּי
‎לֵיל שָׁכְבוֹ אֱלֵי צִדִּי
‎עַל עַרְשִׂי וּמַרְבַדִּי —
‎עַד בֹּקֶר נְשָׁקַנִי
‎וַעֲסִיס פִּיו הֵנִיקַנִי.

‎מַה נֶּחְמָד וְטוֹב דַּרְכּוֹ,
‎מַה מָּתוֹק פְּרִי חִכּוֹ!
‎אַךְ שֶׁקֶר וְרִיק נִסְכּוֹ,
‎הֵתֵל בִּי וְרִמַּנִי,
‎וּבְלִי חֵטְא הֲדָמַּנִי.

‎יוֹם לוֹ כָלְתָה עֵינִי
‎וּלְקוֹל צְלָלָה אָזְנִי,
‎נִחַשְׁתִּי בְּרַב־עֹנִי:
‎כם אחסן לה טני
‎עסי ירגע וידכרני.

‎משה אבן עזרא

·13·

These rivers reveal for the world to see
The secret love concealed in me.

> You who blame me, Ah! be still.
> My love's a stag who's learned to kill,
> Arrogant, with stubborn will.

Passion has disheartened me—
Cruel of him to part from me.

> A fawn is he with slender thighs.
> The sun goes dark when it sees him rise.
> Darts are flying from his eyes.

Stole my sleep away from me,
Altogether wasted me.

> Never will I forget the night
> We lay together in delight
> Upon my bed till morning light.

All night he made love to me,
At his mouth he suckled me.

> Charming even in deceit;
> The fruit of his mouth is like candy sweet.
> Played me false, that little cheat!

Deceived me, then made fun of me;
I did him no wrong, but he wronged me.

> One day when my eyes were filled to the brim
> There came to my ears this little hymn,
> So I sang my doleful song to him:

"How dear that boy is to me!
Maybe he'll come back to me."

Moses Ibn Ezra

·13·

Like the preceding poem, this *muwashshaḥ* uses the personal pronoun "me" as the rhyming syllable in the verses with a constant rhyme. Rhyming in pronouns is often used in the religious poetry of the period to achieve a particular effect; it occurs in the secular poetry as well.[1] Whereas in my translation of poem 12 I dispensed with this original feature, I maintained it here because so much of the meaning and effect of the poem depend upon its stress on the first person.

The individual images and motifs of this poem are routine; the poem's character derives from the way in which these motifs are organized to stress the unifying theme of the lover's isolation. Even fulfilled love isolates the lovers from society by making them both indifferent to their social world and fearful of it. Having bestowed his heart, the lover is vulnerable to total isolation: Should the beloved prove false, he has no one but himself to turn to for comfort. This lover's plight is emphasized by the periodic regularity of the recurring pronoun.

The rivers in the refrain are the lover's tears, which he cannot control. Though uncontrollable weeping, as Ibn Ḥazm tells us, is the very mark of the lover, it is in poor taste because it divulges the secret affair. Since the conventional world regards love itself as being in bad taste, his weeping over its loss is likely to gain the poet more scorn than sympathy. The poet thus has nothing but self-pity to fall back on.

Turning from the speaker's dilemma to the image of the beloved, we find a farrago of paradoxes. The traditional epithet "fawn" is developed into the familiar paradox of the timorous animal wreaking destruction as violently as the most ferocious of animals. Also in accordance with poetic tradition, the deer that is hunted with arrows hunts his lovers with metaphorical arrows. The paradoxes spill over to the lover, who celebrates the slimness of the fawn's thighs but complains of his own emaciation; he nostalgically recalls the sleepless nights of love but laments the sleepless nights of separation. This penchant for opposites is characteristic of Arabic rhetoric; we have already encountered similar ideas in the wine poetry.[2] They remind us that beauty and love occupy a marvelous realm apart from that of ordinary experience, a realm over which individual will and societal pressures have no power. No wonder the poet worries about losing his social equilibrium.

The final couplet of this poem, the *kharja,* is in Arabic; as explained in the introduction, such couplets were ordinarily taken from an actual Arabic poem, of which the Hebrew is an imitation. The quotation from the Arabic model is openly introduced into the Hebrew poem as a quotation, usually in the mouth of another speaker. This poem unfortunately has an unintelligible word just at this crucial spot in the last stanza. The words "so I sang" in the translation stand for a Hebrew word which means "to use divination," an idea that no stretch of my imagination can apply to the context. I conjecture that the original Hebrew word was one which means "to whisper" or "to hum," and that the difficulty arose through the inadvertent miscopying of one letter.[3] The result of the emendation is that the poem ends with the poet telling us about a song that he himself sang on the occasion described. If, as is likely, the Arabic *kharja* belonged to a poem well known to Moses Ibn Ezra's audience, this would have been an effective ending.

‐◡|‐‐◡|‐◡|‐‐◡‐

14

אֵשׁ אַהֲבִים נִשְׁקָה / בִּי — וְאֵיךְ אֶתְאַפְּקָה?

דְּמָתַנִי אַהֲבָה,
כִּי לְיָדִי אֶרְבָּה.
נָפְלָה כְּנֹפֶל שְׁבָא,
בָּחֲרִי אַף דֶּלְקָה, / אֶת לְבָבִי בִּתְּקָה.

יוֹם דְּמָעַי נִגְּרוּ
סוֹד לְבָבִי הֶעֱרוּ.
מַה לְדוֹדִי תֹּאמְרוּ?
אֵין בְּדִמְעָה צְדָקָה / לִי — בְּמָה אֶצְטַדָּקָה?

דַּבְּרוּ לוֹ עַל שְׁמִי
אֶת אֲרֶשֶׁת נָאֲמִי
אַל דָּמִי לָךְ, אַל דֶּמִי!
מִדְוֵה לֵב רָחֲקָה / אַחֲוָה שֶׁנִּתְּקָה.

נַחֲמוּנִי, נַחֲמוּ,
כִּי קְרָבַי יֶהֱמוּ
עַל כְּאֵבִים עָצְמוּ,
וּשְׁנָתִי רָחֲקָה / נְדָדָה גַּם עָתְקָה.

הַלְּבָבוֹת נִתְּקוּ
יֶזְעֲקוּ יִתְחַבְּקוּ,
וּלְבָבִי דָחֲקוּ
לַחֲבֹק — נִתְחַבְּקָה / נִדְבְּקָה נִתְנַשְּׁקָה!

שִׁיר אֲהָבַי מַעֲנֶה
. . . .

שִׁיר יְדִידוֹת תַּעֲנֶה
"עאשקין אעתנקא / רב לא יתפרקא".

שמואל הנגיד

·14·

Burnt by passion's flame—
How can I refrain?
    Love has ruined me,
    Lain in wait for me,
    Ambushed, then gone free
Followed me amain,
Split my heart in twain.

    On my cheek the tear
    Made my secret clear.
    This please tell my dear:
Tears all men disdain.
How can I explain?

    Speak to him for me,
    Tell him of my plea.
    Do not silent be!
Broken love restrain
From a heart in pain.

    Solace to me bring;
    Ease for me the sting.
    Ah, such suffering!
Sleepless have I lain,
Love my slumber's bane.

    Lovers in distress
    Cry for a caress.
    My heart they oppress.
Come my darling swain,
Cling and kiss again.

    This my love song rings
    [   ]
"May true lovers twain
Never part again!"

Samuel the Nagid

·14·

This is another *muwashshaḥ* concluding with an Arabic couplet. The charming rhythm, the interesting *kharja*, and an unusual theme prompt its inclusion, despite the lack of clarity in the penultimate stanza and the loss of a line in the final stanza. The overall sense of the poem is clear enough, and even a modern reader can see why it would have been sufficiently admired to be imitated by another Hebrew poet.[1]

The lover's suffering, uncontrollable weeping, fear of revealing his secret through loss of self-control, and plea to the beloved are all familiar features of love poetry; the poem is atypical in that it belongs to neither the descriptive nor the petitionary types. Like the petitionary poems, it speaks of the poet's broken heart; but unlike them, it includes a suffering beloved. This is a case not of unrequited love but of separation due to outside forces. The lover assumes that the beloved, whom he cannot join, is as unhappy as he.

The rhyme itself affirms the spiritual unity of the lovers. The couplets have the constant rhyme *qa*, which remains semantically neutral until the *kharja*. At this point the rhyme acquires great meaning, for in both halves of this final line the vowel *a* is a grammatical element signifying the dual number. The literal meaning of the *kharja* is: "Two lovers have both embraced— / May the two not be separated."[2] The three-fold use of the dual number is retroactively projected, through the rhyme syllable, on the poem as a whole, lending it a poignancy absent from much of the love poetry.

Since it is not the beloved who is the cause of the lover's pain, it is love itself, to which is attributed the violence usually ascribed to the beloved. The opening stanza is loaded with words of violence: five verbs, four of them in the emphatic rhyme position. The translation of this stanza omits a biblical allusion to the plundering by the Sabeans of Job's flocks, which reinforces the theme of extreme, even proverbial, suffering caused by a violent act.[3]

The separation of the two lovers is not merely accidental but also archetypical, originating in the mythos of love itself. It was commonplace to think of love as resulting from the division of the soul into parts that continually strive to be reunited. Ibn Ḥazm used language similar to that of stanza 5, when he said "Every form always *cries out* for its corresponding form; like is ever at rest with like." [4] This theory had a literary parallel in the standard motif of the spirits of true lovers leaving their bodies during sleep and traversing great distances to enter one another's dreams. Though not explicitly brought into the poem, this motif is implied through the juxtaposition of stanzas 4 and 5. The plea of the *kharja* would then be for an embrace of the spirit in a dream rather than in life, since the poem's premise rules out actual union. It is unfortunate that the lacuna in the last stanza makes it impossible to know exactly how the *kharja* came into the picture.

$$--|-\cup--|--|--\cup--//--|--\cup--|--|--\cup--$$

אָמְנוֹן אֲנִי חוֹלֶה קְראוּ אֱלֵי תָמָר, / כִּי חוֹשְׁקָהּ נָפַל בְּרֶשֶׁת וְגַם מִכְמָר.

רֵעַי, מְיֻדָּעַי, אֵלַי הֲבִיאוּהָ, / אַחַת שְׁאֵלָתִי מִכֶּם אֲשֶׁר אֹמַר:

קִשְׁרוּ עֲטֶרֶת עַל רֹאשָׁהּ, וְהָכִינוּ / עֶדְיָהּ, וְשִׂימוּ עַל יָדָהּ בְּכוֹס חָמָר.

תָּבוֹא וְתַשְׁקֵנִי, אוּלַי תְּכַבֶּה אֵשׁ / לִבִּי, אֲשֶׁר בִּלָּה בְשָׂרִי אֲשֶׁר סָמַר.

שלמה אבן גבירול

·15·

Like Amnon sick am I, so call Tamar
    And tell her one who loves her is snared by death.
Quick, friends, companions, bring her here to me.
    The only thing I ask of you is this:
Adorn her head with jewels, bedeck her well,
    And send along with her a cup of wine.
If she would pour for me she might put out
    The burning pain wasting my throbbing flesh.

Solomon Ibn Gabirol

·15·

Much of Ibn Gabirol's poetry treats standard poetic material in an individual, almost idiosyncratic way, hinting at an unexpectedly dark aspect of a familiar theme. The present poem displays this tendency in connection with love, through a parody of the Bible story of Amnon and Tamar.[1]

Amnon, a son of King David, loved his half-sister, Tamar. On a friend's advice, Amnon feigned illness, then begged their father to send Tamar to cook for him, claiming that this would cure him. Tamar was sent to his bedroom, where Amnon at first tried to seduce her. Failing, he raped and abandoned her.

This is an ugly story, and one wonders why Ibn Gabirol took the risk of strangling his love poem with bad associations. He must have sought something not commonly found in the Bible; and to be sure this is a rare erotic biblical story involving members of the courtly class. The innocent pastoral love of the Song of Songs and the brutal rape of the concubine in Gibeah express different types of feelings.[2] Samson's lusty affairs involve the wrong social class. The story's use of some of the standard elements of secular love poetry, including lovesickness, emaciation, and a lover's confidant offering friendly advice, must have pleased the poet; and perhaps the very horror of the story's outcome attracted him.

The result of superimposing Arabic love poetry on the story of Amnon and Tamar is an ironic piece with a point to make. The action of the Bible story centers on Amnon's ruse, but the poem contains no ruse except one not intended to deceive. Here Amnon's message to his Tamar is to dress as if for a party, to attend him not to prepare medicinal cakes but to relieve his fever by pouring his wine. But in both medieval medicine and poetic imagery wine is hot; like love, it possesses the power to inflame. If the speaker suffers from the fever of love, wine is the last thing he should drink. Tacitly underlying this theme is a famous line by Abu Nuwas to one who reproached him for tippling: "Leave off your blaming; blame makes me rebel / Cure me instead with that which made me ill."[3]

One of the classic medieval anthologies of Arabic love poetry devotes an entire chapter to the absurdity of trying to cure the pain of love with love.[4] Several verses use the image of heaping coals on burning coals. So Ibn Gabirol's audience, as well as his Tamar, were fully aware that a cure for his lovesickness was not what the speaker sought when he sent his friends for her. If she comes, she comes knowingly.

Like Abu Nuwas, the speaker does not want to overcome his sickness but prefers to cultivate it. The Bible story, in one of world literature's most memorable comments on love, tells us exactly how Amnon's love for Tamar ended. When the violence subsided, the story continues, "Then Amnon felt a very great loathing for her; indeed, his loathing for her was greater than the passion he had felt for her."

Thus the reader of this poem, the speaker, his friends, and probably the girl herself, all knew that the consummation of his love for his Tamar would mean the death of the poet's love for her. His pursuit of the affair leads the lover away from it. This irony is the essence of the poem. Love is a game that all parties agree to play by the rules. Though the poem does not explicitly pass judgment on this convention, the sinister echo of Tamar's rape rings quietly but distinctly in the background, a cynical commentary on the conventions of love.

·16·

—— ⌣ — — ⌣ — — ⌣ // — ⌣ — — — ⌣ — — — ⌣

בְּעֵת חֵשֶׁק יְעִירֵנִי, אֲדַלֵּג / כְּאַיָּל לַחֲזוֹת עֵינֵי כְבוּדָּה.

וְאָבוֹאָה — וְהֵן אַמָּה לְנֶגְדָּהּ / וְאָבִיהָ וְאָחִיהָ וְדוֹדָהּ!

אֲשׁוּרֶנָּה — וְאֶפְנֶה לַאֲחוֹרַי, / כְּאִלּוּ לֹא אֲנִי רֵעָהּ יְדִידָהּ,

יָרֵא מֵהֶם, וְעָלֶיהָ לְבָבִי / כְּלֵב אִשָּׁה מְשַׁכֶּלֶת יְחִידָהּ.

יצחק אבן כלפון

·16·

I skip like a gazelle at passion's call
    To see my love, secluded in her hall.
Arriving there, I find my darling in,
    With mother, father, brothers—all her kin.
I take one look and grimly shrink away,
    As if she didn't matter anyway.
Them I fear; but her, my love, I mourn
    Like a mother mourning her first born.

Isaac Ibn Khalfon

This tale of a hapless suitor is only partly in the mainstream of medieval Hebrew love poetry. It accords with tradition in presenting a lover's failure to achieve his desire, but its narrative rather than lyrical presentation puts it in a class by itself. Furthermore, the two personalities of the narrative are not quite in the traditional mold.

The beloved's beauty is not described, nor are her coldness, dangerousness, or any of the qualities on which descriptive love poems dwell. Only one quality is alluded to: She is a woman whose life is spent within her father's home, surrounded by her people, a "fawn of the palace."[1] We know this not only from the situation described in verse 2, which might have been a singular event, but also from the epithet used to refer to the beloved in verse 1. She is called not by any of the standard pet names, but by a word that regularly alludes to the practice in aristocratic families of keeping their women as secluded as possible. The word, *kevudda,* comes from a root that means "honor" or "wealth"; its usage here derives from an ancient Hebrew poem on a royal wedding, preserved in the Bible as Psalm 45, of which verse 16 was understood to mean "All the honor of a princess is that she is kept indoors."[2]

Forced as it seems, this interpretation was a natural one in a world of secluded women. Thus when Ibn Khalfon refers to his lady as *"kevudda,"* we know immediately that she lives her luxurious life mostly within four walls. No matter when a visitor arrived, he would find a scene much like that of verse 2.

Ordinarily we learn about the lover from the way he describes the beloved. Uniquely in this poem, we learn about him by his reference to the beloved's environment, for thus is she, and by inference he, defined. If she is a noble lady sequestered indoors, he is a vagabond, abandoned to the outdoors. It is instructive to watch his progress in the course of the poem. In verse 1 he prances; in verse 2 he arrives; in verse 3 he turns away; and in verse 4 he is reduced to total passivity as motion is replaced by emotion. Her stability appears noble, whereas his motion is futile and hapless. This love poem does not show the poet as beauty's slave; rather, as a buffoon.

This image matches the persona in other poems by Ibn Khalfon, who belonged to the literary type of the Bohemian man of letters, dependent on patronage and living from commission to commission. Many of his poems evoke whimsically the life of a down-and-outer, a precursor of the persona of the more versatile Abraham Ibn Ezra, who wrote:

> If I made shrouds
> No one would die;
> If I sold lamps
> Then in the sky
> The sun for spite
> Would shine at night.[3]

Ibn Khalfon is said to have been the first Hebrew poet of the Golden Age to make his living by poetry.[4] Since he occupied a different social and economic status from our other poets, it is no wonder that the persona he created is also very different.

Just for the sake of completeness, I must mention an ambiguity of the Hebrew language that complicates but does not greatly affect the meaning of the poem. The last member of the family group in verse 2 is the beloved's *dod*. Since this word means "uncle," and it occurs in a list of family members, I understand the poet to have stumbled into a family gathering and translate "kin" for the sake of the rhyme. To me the picture of the lover, the eternal outsider, being intimidated by this intimate gathering and by what it says about his lady's character, is psychologically pointed. But *dod* also means "lover"; accordingly we might translate: "Arriving at her house I find my dove / With mother, father, brothers—and her love." In this version, the lover finds her together with her family and her fiancé, since no other kind of lover could conceivably be admitted to such a group. The poet has arrived too late. I find this interpretation less interesting, but the reader may choose whichever version he prefers.

−∪−│−∪−│−∪−

לֵיל גֻּלְתָה אֵלַי צְבִיָּה נַעֲרָה
חַמַּת לְחָיֶיהָ וְצַמַּת שַׂעֲרָה
צָהֹב — כְּעֵין אֹדֶם בְּכַסּוֹתוֹ עֲלֵי
רַקַּת בְּדֹלַח לַח תְּמוּנַת תָּאֳרָהּ —
דָּמְתָה כְשֶׁמֶשׁ, בַּעֲלוֹתָהּ תַּאֲדִים
אֶת עַנְנֵי נֶשֶׁף בְּלַהַב זָהֳרָהּ.

יהודה הלוי

·17·

The night the girl gazelle displayed to me
    Her cheek—the sun—beneath its veil of hair,
Red as a ruby, and beneath, a brow
    Of moistened marble (color wondrous fair!)
I fancied her the sun, which rising reddens
    Clouds of morning with its crimson flare.

Judah Halevi

This epigram is a highly refined miniature, the kind of poem that has been called an "exquisite trifle." It here displays the technique of poetic craftsmanship practiced by the most skilled medieval Hebrew poets. The exposition must be a bit more technical than usual in order to convey to the non-specialist the nature of the medieval Hebrew poetic craft; but it is possible to explain the poem's mechanics entirely in terms of English grammar and syntax.[1]

Many a love poem begins with a reminiscence of a night of pleasure or sorrow. The night of our poem is recalled because of a provocative gesture on the part of the beloved. The opening leads us to expect an action answering to the character of her initiating action; but the answering gesture is completely internal, nothing more than a figure of speech, a simile in the mind of the poet. The poet's artistic response balances evenly against the stimulation of the beloved's beauty-revealing gesture. This is achieved by management of the poem's syntax.

The poem is one long sentence spread over three verses, with the verb at the beginning of verse 3. Although enjambment is not as rare in Arabic and Hebrew poetry as medieval handbooks and most modern studies would lead one to expect, the poet has gone out of his way to stress it. One way he does this is by placing the adjective here translated "red" at the beginning of verse 2, forcing the performer to continue without pausing between verses. But the whole character of the Arabic prosody adopted by the Hebrew poets depends on the regular rise and fall of verses that are exactly even in length and punctuated by rhyme. Reading the two verses together obscures the resolution and creates a tension that is heightened syntactically by delaying the main clause until verse 3. The verb at the beginning of this verse, which signals the arrival of the long-awaited resolution, is thus in a highly stressed position; this gives the feeling that the poet's artistic response in verse 3 balances the action of the beloved in verses 1 and 2.

The words in verse 1 that denote the girl's cheek and hair are identical but for one consonant. Experience with the rhetoric of this poetry and its love of contrasts leads us to expect that the poet will develop the juxtaposition, and the same experience leads us to expect that he will contrast the light color of her cheek with the darkness of her hair. The poet does indeed go on to speak of colors, but instead of contrasting, he unifies them with a simile. We are surprised, because we expect the hair to be black; we learn that it is red at the beginning of verse 2, through that same adjective with an obscure antecedent that causes so much syntactic tension.

It helps, but is not necessary, to know that light-colored hair came into fashion among Andalusian poets during the eleventh century.[2] The important point is that our expectation of a description based on contrasts has been thwarted; instead we are given a more subtle coordination of colors, amounting to a small *tour de force*. The colors associated with the girl's beauty negate the color that the reader automatically associates with the poem's first word, "night."

Though the brilliance of the girl's red hair and glowing complexion remind the poet of the sun, that does not mean that the girl is warm. Her hair is a veil, a separator, and it is compared to a stone, which for all its color is an inanimate object. The cheek is compared to another stone, originally crystal rather than the marble of the translation. I changed the name of the stone in order to imitate the play of sounds in the Hebrew, which reads "*bedolakh lakh*," or moist crystal, believing that the alliteration here is more important than the exact stone. The image reinforces the picture of the girl's character by calling attention to the brightness, coolness, and perhaps even slipperiness of the stone's surface. When, in the next verse, the imagery turns to the rising sun, the image of stones is so well established that we are able to imagine a sun that has radiance but no warmth—exactly the way the poet projects the girl.

·18·

```
——|—◡——|—◡——//——|——|—◡——|—◡——
```

יוֹם שֶׁעֲשַׁעְתִּיהוּ עֲלֵי בִרְכַּי / וַיַּרְא תְּמוּנָתוֹ בְּאִישׁוֹנִי,

נָשַׁק שְׁתֵּי עֵינַי עֵינֵי מְחַעְתֵּעַ — / אֶת תָּאֲרוֹ נָשַׁק וְלֹא עֵינָי!

יהודה הלוי

(תרגום משיר ערבי מאת אלמתנבי)

·18·

Once when I fondled him upon my thighs
    He caught his own reflection in my eyes
And kissed my eyes, deceitful imp; I knew
    It was his image he kissed, and not my eyes!

Judah Halevi,
translation from the Arabic original by al-Mutanabbi

·18·

Here is another reminiscence, this time of a daytime scene, and again the center of attention is the heartless beloved. The mood of the lover is not at all bitter, for both lovers are knowingly engaged in a game. Even this tiny epigram is able both to describe the event and to catch its mood through manipulation of language. The word translated "deceitful" could express bitter denunciation, were it not matched by another word of the same distinctive pattern, meaning "played." The deception is part of the play; so too the beloved's narcissism. The lover is not criticizing the beloved but expressing satisfaction that she plays the game so well.

·19·

——◡|———◡|———◡

שְׁלוֹמוֹתַי מְסוּכִים בַּדְּמָעוֹת

שְׂאוּ הָרִים וְקִרְאוּ הַגְּבָעוֹת

לְעֵינַיִם בְּבַת עֵינִי קְרוּעוֹת

וְאֶצְבָּעוֹת בְּדַם לִבִּי צְבוּעוֹת

וְאִם לֹא אֲהֵבָתַהּ לִי תְּעִירוּן

תְּעִירוּן רַחֲמֶיהָ לַדְּמָעוֹת

יהודה הלוי

·19·

Bear my greetings, mixed with tears,
    Mountains, hills—whoever hears—
To ten lovely fingernails
    Painted with blood from my entrails;
To eyes mascaraed with black dye
    From the pupil of my eye.
Though she'll never call me dear,
    Maybe she'll pity me for my tear.

Judah Halevi

·19·

This little poem, with its startling image in verse 2, is a highly con-
centrated rendition of the feelings and attitudes typical of petition-
ary love poetry.

Unable to address his beloved directly, the poet appeals to fea-
tures of the landscape to convey his greetings. We are not told why
he cannot greet her in person. The second verse suggests that she is
too dangerous to approach; the third, that she is indifferent. Per-
haps the true reason is implied by the first verse, in which the
reader's eyes are drawn upward to the mountains and hills. Lofty
messengers are needed to carry the message to a still loftier object.
Here is the classic statement in Hebrew of the lover's humility.

The image of the beloved using the lover's blood to stain her fin-
gertips (the fingertips, rather than the fingernails, were stained) is
a common one. Blood may be used because that is what the lover
weeps instead of tears. The same way of thinking makes the black
of the eye or even the liver's bile available as mascara.

·20·

—◡—|—◡——|—◡——

עׇפְרָה תְכַבֵּס אֶת בְּגׇדֶיהָ בְּמֵי
דְמׇעִי וְתִשְׁטָחֵם לְשֶׁמֶשׁ זׇהֳרָהּ,
לֹא שָׁאֲלָה מֵי הָעֲיׇנוֹת — עִם שְׁתֵּי
עֵינַי, וְלֹא שֶׁמֶשׁ — לִיפִי תׇאֳרָהּ.

יהודה הלוי

·20·

Ofra does her laundry with my tears
    And spreads it out before her beauty's rays.
With my two eyes she needs no flowing well;
    Nor sun needs she: Her face provides the blaze.

Judah Halevi

Ofra, the Hebrew word for a female fawn, regularly denotes the beloved; here it is used as a proper noun. The epigram is built on images of complementary actions. The lover contributes his adoration, the beloved, her beauty; but the picture is not quite symmetrical, for it is to *her* cause that they both contribute. The theme is really the same as the theme of blood for henna and pupil for mascara in the preceding poem; the lover's adoration enhances the desirability of the beloved.

Less important to the poem's effect but noteworthy is a pun in the Hebrew on the word *ʿayin,* which serves for both "eye" and "well." The comparison of the beloved's face with the sun almost attributes warmth to her; but because it is a utilitarian warmth, suitable for drying laundry, the hard-heartedness of the beloved is sustained.

The medieval collection of Halevi's poems has this heading preceding the epigram: "He passed by a beautiful washer-woman and said, improvising . . ." The sight of slave girls, some of them beautiful, doing laundry in a brook or well must have been a familiar, charming sight in medieval Andalusia. Perhaps this epigram refers to a sensational true anecdote involving a laundress and poetic improvisation. Al-Muʿtamid, prince of Seville from 1069 to 1090, was walking with his friend and Minister Ibn ʿAmmar along the Guadalquivir. Noticing how the river was rippled by the wind, the prince challenged Ibn ʿAmmar with the improvised hemistich "Behold a breastplate welded by the breeze."

Ibn ʿAmmar was unable to complete the couplet, but a slave girl working at her laundry overheard their conversation and broke in with "And fitted for the warrior, would it freeze." [1]

Al-Muʿtamid was so impressed with her wit that he bought, freed, and married her. She became one of the most pampered princesses of her time.

·21·

—— | ᴗ —— | — ᴗ — | — ᴗ —— // — | — ᴗ —— | — ᴗ — | — ᴗ ——

אֵלִי, הֲפָךְ נָא לְבַב גּוֹזָל אֲשֶׁר גָּזַל / נוּמִי — וְיָשִׁיב לְעַפְעַפַּי מְעַט שֵׁנָה.

אָהוּב אֲשֶׁר בָּא בְּאָלָתָךְ וְנָתַן לִי / אַהְבַת לְבָבוֹ בְּלִי אוֹנֶס בְּמַתָּנָה—

בָּגַד וְכֵן כָּל צְבִי בוֹגֵד, וְעַתָּה אִם / תִּשָּׂא לְחֶטְאוֹ, וְאִם אַיִן — מְחֵנִי נָא!

שמואל הנגיד

·21·

Change, my God, the heart of that chick that checked
    My sleep, and make him give it back to me;
A fawn who swore by Your name to give
    His love to me, a gift of his own free will,
And then betrayed me; lovers all betray.
    Forgive his sin—or wipe me out, I pray.

Samuel the Nagid

·21·

The unusual designation of the beloved as "chick" appears to be an experiment in the development of Hebrew terminology parallel to that of Arabic. Love poems are called *ghazal* in Arabic, which was understood as being related to *ghazāl,* the word for gazelle that became a standard designation of the beloved. Whereas the Arabic word for deer (*ẓaby*) has a cognate in Hebrew (*ṣevi*), the Arabic word for gazelle does not; it does however sound very much like the Hebrew *gozal,* meaning "young dove," which is the word used here. This usage did not become standardized. Here it is part of a pun, for the phrase translated "chick that checked my sleep" means literally "young dove (*gozal*) that stole (*gazal*) my sleep."

"Forgive his sin, or wipe me out" at the climax of the poem echoes Exodus 32:32, in which Moses petitioned God on behalf of the Israelites after the incident of the Golden Calf.

·22·

```
— — ◡ | — — — ◡ | — — — ◡ / / — — ◡ | — — — ◡ | — — — ◡
```

יְשׁוּרֵנִי וְעַפְעַפּוֹ כְּחוֹלֶה / וְהַכּוֹס מִדְּמוּת לֶחְיוֹ מְמֻלָּא,
וְנִיבָיו מִשְּׂפָתָיו דַּר עֲלֵי דַר, / וּבִשְׂחוֹק פִּיו בְּכֶתֶם לֹא יְסֻלֶּה.
וְהַנִּיבוֹת אֲשֶׁר בָּם יְקְטְלֵנִי / כְּנִיב נוֹשֶׂה עֲלֵי אִישׁ רָשׁ וְנִקְלֶה.
וְהַכּוֹס רָץ כְּשֶׁמֶשׁ בַּשְּׁחָקִים, / וְהַיּוֹם נָד נְדוֹד רֵעִים וְגוֹלֶה,
וְדָמִי יַעֲרֹף עָלַי וְנִבְהַל / עֲלֵי לֶחְיִי — וְלֹא יוֹרֵד וְעוֹלֶה!

שלמה אבן גבירול

·22·

He watches me, his eyelids like an invalid's;
      The goblet with the likeness of his cheek is filled;
Behind his lips, his teeth are pearl on pearl;
      He smiles with a mouth more precious far than gold,
His every tooth a word that murders me,
      Like a pitiless creditor dunning a penniless wretch.
The goblet goes round like the sun in the sky;
      The day is departing: so friends disappear.
My blood is raining all over me, rushing
      Down on my cheek, to go up no more.

Solomon Ibn Gabirol

Though this difficult poem contains many of the clichés of Golden Age love poetry, it has the Gabirolian individuality we have already noted; its tone and attitude are very different from anything else in this anthology, and, for that matter, from the rest of the literature. Even a first-time reader will notice that the witty paradoxes characteristic of this poetry are completely absent and that the poem is built on a series of bizarre comparisons. Its ending is strangely inconclusive, its emotional atmosphere tragic.

The poem presupposes a situation already quite familiar to us. The poet is at a drinking party contemplating a beautiful boy, probably the *sáki*. This is the time of the poet's heightened consciousness, when other drinkers have faded out and his own specially attuned feelings are at work, perceiving things imperceptible to others.

The first three verses describe the boy; the last two describe the circumstances. The first three verses describe static objects, whereas the objects mentioned in the last two verses are in motion.[1] This division is strengthened by the syntactic rhythm of the first three verses. Verses 1 and 2 have a different item to describe in each hemistich, and a different grammatical subject and predicate in each; verse 3, with its more expansive disposition of a single subject in the first hemistich and a single predicate in the second, creates a sense of repose. Whereas there is nothing intrinsically energetic about the rhythm of verses 1 and 2, the return of their syntactic rhythm in verse 4 has the effect of putting the poem back into motion after stasis.[2]

According to the poem's opening words, it is the boy who is looking at the speaker; but it is the speaker's observations that the poem goes on to describe. From the statement in verse 4 that the cup is still being passed around, we may infer that others are still awake; but poet and boy occupy a small space with just enough room for the two of them, and within this space they gaze languidly at one another.

Interaction does not come naturally to the boy. His eyelids are heavy, like a sick man's: sick with illness? sick with wine? or sick with love? The poem raises the question without answering it directly. All we know is that there is wine in his cup and that it resembles his cheek in color. Latent in the simile is the notion that this medieval Narcissus is drunk with, or in love with, his own beauty. As the languor grows on him his eyes become heavier and heavier and he turns more and more inward. From this point on it is the speaker who is doing all the looking.

He concentrates on the boy's mouth in a progression from tangible to intangible, from teeth to smile to speech. All three are connected by similes to images of wealth: teeth to pearls, smile to gold, speech—most unexpectedly—to a creditor. The first two images were morally neutral and conventionally beautiful; the third is morally suspect and emotionally shocking. The Hebrew word *niv* used for "speech" is a homonym of the word for "teeth" in verse 2, so the lovely rows of pearls have turned into lethal fangs (this is the meaning of the Arabic cognate). Thus the word *niv* is the pivot on which the poem turns from admiration to despair. The verse is rhythmically static, ending the description of the boy; but thematically it is dynamic, opening a whole new subject with its shocking theme and perplexing simile.

The goblet goes around the circle of drinkers borne by the *sáki*. The comparison with the sun is apt, for the wine in the goblet diminishes as it goes, to be replenished from the jug and started again on its cycle. The poet's thoughts shift from the wine to the setting of the real sun, which in turn brings to mind thoughts of loss and separation. As the thought of irrevocable loss alters the emotional content of the imagery, the cyclical motion of the cup modulates into the linear motion of loss, ending in the grotesque metaphor in verse 5.

We have already had several examples of the use of blood for tears, but its use here is so abrupt, direct, and downright ugly that we have no choice but to reflect on its meaning as if it were a newly invented figure of speech.

Frustrated lovers regularly weep blood, in the standard image; here the context and choice of words add unusual nuances. The verb translated "raining" carries with it overtones of its homonym, which means "to cut someone's throat"; if the falling fluid had simply been "tears," which would fit the meter perfectly, this association might not have occurred to anyone, but since the poet has introduced the image of blood for tears he must have welcomed this additional gruesome reinforcement. Falling tears, dripping rain, blood from a cut throat are all in linear motion, which connotes irreversible loss. Thinking for a moment of the *visual* effect of the image of falling tears as dripping blood, we realize that the poet's tear-stained cheek appears blood-stained. This may be literally true, for his cheeks would be flushed from drinking. But this is not the first wine-red cheek in the poem; the whole scene began with the face of the boy reflected in the wine. The speaker and the boy, the despairing lover and the narcissistic beauty, thus mirror one another. One is red with the symbol of beauty and joy, the other with the symbol of mortality.

To summarize: The boy, who occupies the first half of the poem, is connected with themes of wealth, stasis, and equipoise; he is the focus of the description, and the items described are all part of him. The speaker is merely one of the items in the environment described in the second half of the poem. He is connected with themes of motion, poverty, and loss. The boy, embodiment of external beauty, looks inward; the poet, embodiment of profound understanding, looks outward. The boy is languorous; the poet, agonized.

Thus does the poetry of wine and women prepare us for the poetry of death.

3 Death

We have had several occasions to observe the charming picture of the poet musing over his cups about the perishability of worldly beauty. Though beguiled by the pleasures of the wine party and all that it represents, unlike his fellows he is not completely taken in.

In this setting, the poet offers his auditors advice, usually a variation on the ancient saying, "*Carpe diem,*" or "Seize the day." His mood is mellow, and his advice is usually given gently. He is knowing, but not authoritarian. He does not speak as master to disciple, but almost as if addressing himself. He is rueful, not bitter. He is aware of the brevity of life and has learned to accept it.

Death is treated in several other poetic genres. One that had great social importance in the Golden Age was the formal lament for the dead, really a special case of the panegyric *qaṣida,* distinguished by characteristics appropriate to its function. Of course, such poems contain expressions of sorrow over the individual whose passing they lament. But they also contain reflections on the brevity of life, drawn from a stock of common gnomic motifs and applied to the particular situation.[1] Because of their public character, such laments are formal in tone and often impersonal.

They probably did not provide an adequate outlet for deeply felt personal grief, since several poets composed poems of lament not belonging to the genre at all, and these poems are much more touching. One of this kind has been included in the anthology.

From the Arabs, the Jewish poets inherited another poetic genre in which thoughts of death play a great part. These are the *zuhdiyat*, sermon-like poems preaching asceticism. The Arab poet most closely associated with the genre is one of the famous poets of the Abbasid period, Abu ʾl-ʿAtahiya (748–825), who is to ascetic poetry what Abu Nuwas is to wine poetry. The two men were acquainted and are said to have agreed not to encroach on one another's preferred theme.[2] Much of Abu ʾl-ʿAtahiya's poetry is obsessed with death. In light of the end in store for every man, the petty activities and desires that occupy most people seem trivial; a person should devote his life to repentance and good works, renouncing all pleasures. The speaker's tone is authoritarian and relentlessly harsh.

His message is, of course, the opposite of that of the wine poet. It derives from a very different social institution: the sermons of popular preachers, emotional harangues that horrified and entertained crowds of the uneducated faithful, and which ultimately go back to the doom-filled eschatological visions of the Quran. Yet specifically Islamic doctrine is not prominent in the writings of Abu ʾl-ʿAtahiya. Though his poetry contains numerous references to resurrection, Paradise, and Hell, he was accused by his contemporaries of heresy, specifically of denying these cardinal principles of Islam.[3] His contemporaries may have perceived that his rejection of the things of this world was too extreme to be consonant with Mohammad's religion, and that ultimately it was not an Islamic ideal that Abu ʾl-ʿAtahiya preached. It has been said that Abu ʾl-ʿAtahiya "diluted the specifically Muslim message into a general monotheistic gnomic."[4] It may be this feature of his work that led to accusations of heresy against him; it may also be that this feature of his poetry made him one Muslim religious writer who appealed to Jews. One does not need to be a Muslim to be moved by verses such as the following:

> Bear sons for death, build homes for ruin.
> You are all going toward destruction.

> For whom do we build, when we to dust
> >   Return, as we were made of dust?
> O Death! I see no escape from you.
> >   You come, with no injustice or preferment.
> You seem to pounce upon my gray hair
> >   Just as gray hair pounced upon my youth.
> . . . .[5]

Abu 'l-ʿAtahiya's poetry is founded on common human experience. His poetic style is extremely simple. By avoiding poetic vocabulary and elaborate rhetoric, it gains intensity through directness. It helped to establish gnomic poetry as part of the Arabic poet's repertoire, joining the poetry of wine and love among the minor genres. By the middle of the tenth century, when the Andalusian Jews began to imitate the literary fashions of the Arabs, gnomic poetry had become naturalized among the genres of classical Arabic poetry, and the Jews adopted it as readily as they did the other genres.

Samuel the Nagid set the standard in this, as in other aspects of Golden Age poetry. His gnomic poetry was collected in two large volumes, one of them, edited by his son, entitled *The Little Book of Proverbs,* the other called *The Little Book of Ecclesiastes.*[6] The former is devoted to social and political maxims; the latter, to meditations on life, old age, and death. Moses Ibn Ezra devoted a chapter of his *ʿAnaq* to gnomic themes, among chapters devoted to wine parties, *sákis,* and gardens.[7] Like the other great poets of the age, he also wrote many independent poems on death.

Even in the fictional poetry-improvising contests described in the *Taḥkemoni,* gnomic poetry plays a part. The twenty-two homonym-poems with which an unknown sheikh, in a story partially quoted earlier in this book, displays his mastery at the expense of the younger contestants are all gnomic poems.[8] Thus these poems have the same social context as that which produced poems on wine and on other items of luxury and amusement.

All this implies that the culture of educated Jews, like that of educated Muslims, included conventional seriousness as well as conventional frivolity. Their life of pleasure was not one of dissipation, but a balanced life of aristocratic elegance. "The serious" and "the flippant" are even categories in Arabic rhetoric, and the artful combination of the two was as admired in poetry as it was in life.

Unlike the poetry of wine drinking and of love, the poetry of death has ample precedent in the Hebrew religious tradition. Religion is one of the main systems devised by man to regulate his anxiety about death, and the Jewish calendar provided the liturgical poet with opportunities to express these feelings on behalf of the community. An anonymous masterpiece still found in the Ashkenazic liturgy for Rosh Hashana and Yom Kippur does this in perfectly simple Hebrew, making use of anaphora:

> On Rosh Hashana they are written,
> And on Yom Kippur they are sealed:
> How many will vanish away,
> And how many will be given being;
> Who will live, and who will die;
> Who in his time, and who untimely;
> Who by fire, and who by water;
> Who by sword, and who by beast;
> Who by famine, and who by drought;
> Who by earthquake, and who by plague;
> Who by strangling, and who by stoning;
> . . . .[9]

The liturgical poet does not compose out of pure aestheticism. He has a message. Like an artist, he manipulates language in order to release feelings in his congregation; but like a teacher, he uses those feelings to make a point. The lesson is the purpose of his writing, and feelings are subordinated to it. In the passage just quoted, the poet speaks of what men fear most: death, and the unexpected ways it may find them. The subject is frightening, and the seemingly endless list of possibilities couched in a relentless duple meter arouses the congregation to ecstatic horror. After establishing the duple meter, the poet abruptly shifts into triple meter for his message:

> But repentance, prayer, and charity
> Cancel the harsh decree.

Through the rhythmic change, the poet moves the congregation to *feel* the efficacy of repentance. His artistry is in the service of his message, preparing the minds of the congregants for the words of guidance and admonition that are his real point.

This purpose of educating the worshipper to a life of piety gave rise to an entire genre of liturgical poetry, the *tokheḥa,* or poem of rebuke. This genre, a kind of versified sermon incorporated into the Yom Kippur liturgy, was cultivated throughout the history of liturgical poetry, including the Golden Age. At the heart of many of these poems is the saying reported by the Mishna, composed in Roman Palestine:

> ʿAqavia ben Mahalalel says: Reflect upon three things and you will not fall into the power of sin. Know whence you have come, and where you are going, and to whom you will one day render account. Whence have you come? From a fetid drop [of semen]. Where are you going? To a place of dirt, maggots, and worms. And to whom will you render account? To the King of Kings, the Holy One, Blessed is He.[10]

Most of the *tokheḥot* do not develop the macabre possibilities of this statement, though they do draw from it the idea that a man should live in continual consciousness of his mortality, so that all his actions will be directed toward self-improvement.[11] The speaker in such poems stands apart, addressing his audience with advice drawn from his own deeper wisdom. This orientation is remarkable, in view of the fact that the speaker in liturgical poetry is the cantor, who, as the congregation's spokesman before God, normally addresses Him rather than his principals. This clash between the function of liturgical poetry and the contents of the *tokheḥa* reflects the origin of the latter in the sermon and, ultimately, in the common wisdom literature of the ancient near East.

Except for the preaching of the *tokheḥa,* synagogue poets did not devote much attention to death. Their concern was with the people as a whole, rather than the individual. They deal in eschatology, savoring the vision of the collapse of the wicked empires who subjugate Israel, and the restoration of Israel to its land; the projected joy of the righteous at beholding God's radiant presence, and the discomfiture of the wicked at the moment when they have no choice but to admit, like Pharaoh, "The Lord is righteous and I and my people are sinners." It is the national fate and Israel's covenant with God that concern the synagogue poet. As for the *tokheḥa,* it may be distinguished from the secular gnomic poem on death by a simple criterion. Because of their didactic function, *tokhehot* end by telling the audience what to *do* (i.e., repent); whereas if secular death poems offer any instruction at all, it is on how to *feel*.

The nexus of the secular and liturgical poems on death is well observed in an unusual *tokheha* by Abraham Ibn Ezra.[12] In ten stanzas, this liturgical poem surveys the ages of man's life as a tale of progressive decay. The early years are vividly rendered: The five-year-old child rides on his father's back; the ten-year-old is so charming that no one has the heart to scold him; the twenty-year-old "leaps like a gazelle" (an image we have come to know from the love poetry[13]) and ignores his teachers. But the thirty-year-old is trapped by responsibility; the forty-year-old is resigned to having his life completely focused on work; the fifty-year-old begins to think of death. At sixty man's physical powers wane; by seventy (if he lives that long) he is a nuisance; at eighty a helpless burden; and after that, as good as dead. The poem concludes: "Happy is he who realizes that he is a sojourner [in life], / Who has no idea or thought in his heart / But for his soul's end and his reward."

The moral of this liturgical poem is simply tacked onto the end; clearly the poet's enthusiasm has all gone into the first nine stanzas. This *tokheha* is really a secular gnomic poem with a vague religious sentiment added. It slipped into the synagogue because it shares a theme with the *tokheha* genre. But the sheer fun of this poem so overbalances its practical religious instruction that it is incongruous in its liturgical environment.

Viewed in this way, the poem displays not so much the piety of the community that produced it as its materialism and secularity. There have been communities—Jewish, Muslim, and Christian— that thrilled to the horrific visions of divine wrath offered by preachers and liturgical poets, and whose religious rites aroused them to frenzies of contrition and remorse. When Abraham Ibn Ezra's *tokheha* was recited in the synagogue, the congregation enjoyed a witty survey of their own lives, half devoted to the robust pleasures of youth and half to regret (almost bitterness) at their decline.

Discussing the poetry of mortality composed in western Europe of the late medieval period, J. Huizinga wisely observed:

> A thought which so strongly attaches to the earthly side of death can hardly be called truly pious . . . [T]hese preachers of

contempt for the world express, indeed, a very materialistic senti-
ment, namely, that all beauty and all happiness are worthless *be-
cause* they are bound to end soon.[14]

This reasoning applies to much of the gnomic poetry of the courtier-
rabbis, which fundamentally is no less secular than their poetry on
wine and on love. Huizinga's remark that "the pious exhortations
to think of death and the profane exhortations to make the most of
youth almost meet" exactly fits the culture here described.

The wealthy, powerful, and worldly men who produced Golden
Age poetry had much to lose, and they had all seen men like them-
selves lose it. The garden, the symbol of their ideal world, repre-
sented through its seasonal cycle the vicissitudes of courtly life and
life in general. Their celebration of the garden's joys is often
touched with melancholy. Thus, for the last time, we begin our se-
lection of poems with a garden in spring.

DEATH

— ‿ ‿ | ‿ ‿ ‿ | ‿ ‿ ‿ ‿ / ‿ ‿ | ‿ ‿ ‿ ‿ / ‿ ‿ | ‿ ‿ ‿ ‿ ‿

זְמָן הַקֹּר כְּצֵל בָּרַח, וְגִשְׁמוֹ / כְּבָר חָלַף וּפָרָשָׁיו וְרִכְבּוֹ,

וְחָל שֶׁמֶשׁ בְּרֹאשׁ טָלֶה, עֲלֵי חֹק / תְּקוּפָתוֹ, כְּמֶלֶךְ עַל מְסִבּוֹ,

וְחָבְשׁוּ מִגְבְּעוֹת צִצִּים גְּבָעוֹת / וּמִישׁוֹר — כֻּתֳּנוֹת דְּשָׁאוֹ וְעֶשְׂבּוֹ,

יְשַׁלַּח אֶל נְחִירֵינוּ קְטֹרֶת / יְמוֹתֵי הַסְּתָו טָמַן בְּחֵבּוֹ.

תְּנָה הַכּוֹס, אֲשֶׁר יָשִׁיר מְשׁוֹשִׁי / וְיָסִיר מִלְּבָבִי מַעֲצָבוֹ,

וְכַבֵּה אֶת יְקוֹד אִשּׁוֹ בְּדִמְעִי, / לְמַעַן כִּי חֲמָתוֹ בָּעֲרָה בוֹ.

וְגוּר מֵהַזְּמָן כִּי מַתְּנוֹתָיו / כְּרֹאשׁ פֶּתֶן מְעַט נֹפֶת בְּקִרְבּוֹ

וְהַשִּׂיא נַפְשְׁךָ בֹּקֶר בְּטוּבוֹ — / וְיָחֵל תַּהֲפוּכוֹתָיו בְּעַרְבּוֹ!

שְׁתֵה בַיּוֹם — עֲדֵי יִפֶן וְשֶׁמֶשׁ / עֲלֵי כַסְפּוֹ יְצַפֶּה אֶת זְהָבוֹ,

וּבַלַּיְלָה — עֲדֵי יִבְרַח כְּשָׁחוֹר / וְיַד שַׁחַר מְאַחֵז אֶת עֲקֵבוֹ.

משה אבן עזרא

·23·

December's frost has fled like shadows; gone
       Are Winter's rains, his horse and cavaliers.
The sun has come around to Ares' head,
       Alighted there and settled on his throne.
The hills are wearing hats bedecked with buds;
       The valley has on vests of grass and herbs,
Releasing fragrances for us to sense,
       Throughout the winter hidden deep inside.

Pass round the cup which makes my joy to rule,
       And roots out sorrow from my aching heart;
And spill the waters of my tears to quench
       Its flames that burn so hot within.
Beware of Time: the gifts that he bestows
       Are venom mixed with honey to taste sweet.
Beguile yourself at morning with his joys,
       But know that they will vanish with the sun.

So drink by day till sunset washes the silver with golden light,
And drink in the dark till dawn puts all his negro troops to flight.

Moses Ibn Ezra

DEATH

Though longer, more complex, and more subtle, our opening poem on death shares several themes and its three-part structure with poem 9. The poem opens with the change from winter to spring, follows with a call to drink wine on the newly verdant lawn, and concludes with sad thoughts aroused by the change of season. Though it really belongs to the genre of wine poetry, the dark consciousness of death so colors all three parts of the poem that it seems an appropriate opening to this section.

The depiction of the changing season as the reinstatement of a king is familiar from the first poem in this anthology. Here, the hillside is turned out in finery to greet the sun, in celebration not of his release from prison, but of his victory in battle with the forces of winter. Care is taken, especially in verse 2, to use words that suggest regular, cyclical recurrence. Without going into philological detail, I may mention, for example, that the word here translated "throne" is derived from a root that means "to go round" and probably originally designated a couch or mat on which participants in a banquet would sit, these mats being arranged in a circle. The word is used in the Song of Songs of a king: "While the king was on his couch, my nard gave forth its fragrance."[1] The second half of the quotation suggests the idea of fragrance, thus linking this verse in the reader's mind with the next.

The alliterations in verse 3 are intended to represent word plays in the Hebrew that are significant less as witticisms than as preparation for other rhetorical tricks. They set up a correspondence between things and their names, a feeling of harmony between natural entities and the forms men use to describe them. They also affirm rhetorically the feeling that things are in their proper places—the sun on his kingly throne, and the hills bedecked to greet him. If the poem ended here, these puns and the parallel balancing of the line would enforce a sense of closure.[2]

But the poem does not end here. The loosely attached circumstantial clause that follows in verse 4 turns our attention to another world lying beneath the neatly settled, balanced surface world of hills and hats, valleys and vests. The fragrance now investing that harmonious world had lain deep inside the earth throughout winter. The distinctive Hebrew phrase here translated "hidden deep inside" carries over from its source in the Book of Job associations of concealed guilt and consciousness of sin hidden from the world, associations as immaterial and as palpable as the fragrance of spring.[3] Together with the intentionally weakened closure rhythm in verse 3, it brings the first thematic part of the poem to an uncertain, foreboding end.

In the middle section, rhetorical tricks and ambiguous grammatical relationships serve to develop the anxiety adumbrated by the phrase from Job. It was not possible to find English equivalents for all of them, and it is particularly unfortunate that the play on words that serves as a structural pivot for the whole poem could only be hinted at in the translation. The Hebrew verb in the phrase "makes my joy to rule" (*yaśir*) is a perfect homophone of the verb in the phrase "roots out sorrow" (*yasir*). The first of these verbs, *yaśir*, meaning "to make rule," is an exceedingly rare word. It is intelligible because it is derived from a familiar root, but it occurs only once in the Bible.[4] Since the second verb, *yasir*, meaning "to remove," has been a rather common word at all periods of the language's history, it is the one that the audience would automatically think of upon first hearing the verse. They must have been puzzled at first, for they could only have understood the sentence as meaning "Pass round the cup that takes away my joy."

Only after second thoughts, reinforced by the unambiguous words, "And removes (*yasir*) from my heart its sorrow" in the second hemistich, would they have retroactively grasped the poet's meaning. He has created this confusion deliberately, and underlined it with a row of hissing sibilants to let the reader sense his ambiguous feelings about the pleasures he is apparently celebrating.

Wine was ordinarily mixed with water in the Middle Ages as it was in antiquity, giving rise to the image, common in love poetry, of wine mixed with tears.[5] But what flames are to be quenched by the tears that the poet orders poured in verse 5? Does he want to dilute the wine so as to diminish its flame? Or does he want to alleviate the flaming sorrow of his heart by pouring tears on it? In either case he is grieving. And since tears themselves are hot, he pursues for relief what can only aggravate his sorrow. Grammatical ambiguity here obscures details but brilliantly reveals one of the poem's main points: that for the truly sensitive man, the standard method of assuaging sorrow only makes it worse.

The following verse contains another untranslatable device, this time an anagram linking the roots for honey (*nft*) and the venom of serpents (*ptn*). The pleasures of life are not mere illusions; they harbor mortal danger. The venom-producing serpent is linked with the serpent of Paradise by means of the verb "beguile" in verse 8. This is a relatively uncommon word, familiar mainly from the words of Eve, "The serpent duped me, and I ate."[6] The fruit that Eve was beguiled into eating was the fruit of the Tree of Knowledge of Good and Evil. Her lapse brought death into the world. The pleasures with which life beguiles the reveler are the pleasures of ignorance, of looking away from the truth about life, a lapse into death of the soul.

The poet is not a moralist, and his purpose is not to counsel against life's pleasures. He is an artist whose purpose is to express exquisitely ambiguous sensations. Spring is not a linear motion in time, like a victory in war; it is part of a cyclical motion, like a king's annual progress. If spring comes, winter cannot be far behind. And nature's flourishing is not only a majestic, slow-paced annual cycle of growth and decay but also a daily cycle, from sunrise to sunset; this more rapid motion better symbolizes man's feeling about the duration of life and worldly joys. The end of the poem takes its imagery from the daily, rather than annual, motion of the sun, and the final image of fleeing soldiers makes us feel acutely how little time we have to enjoy life.

‍‎－－－◡｜－－－◡｜－◡／｜－－－◡｜－－－◡｜－◡

אֲצַפֶּה אֱלֵי שַׁחַק וְכוֹכָבָיו — / וְאַבִּיט בְּאֶרֶץ אֶת רְמָשֶׂיהָ,
וְאָבִין בְּלִבִּי כִּי יְצִירָתָם / יְצִירָה מְחֻכָּמָה בְּמַעֲשֶׂיהָ.
רְאוּ אֶת שְׁמֵי מָרוֹם כְּמוֹ קֻבָּה / תְּפוּרִים בְּלוּלָאוֹת קְרָסֶיהָ,
וְסַהַר וְכוֹכָבָיו כְּמוֹ רוֹעָה / תְּשַׁלַּח בְּתוֹךְ אָחוּ כְּבָשֶׂיהָ,
כְּאִלּוּ לְבָנָה בֵּין נְשִׂאֵי עָב / סְפִינָה מְהַלֶּכֶת בְּנִסֶּיהָ,
וְעָנָן כְּצַלְמָה עַל פְּנֵי גִנָּה / תְּהַלֵּךְ וְתַשְׁקֶה אֶת הֲדַסֶּיהָ,
וְעָב טַל כְּמוֹ נַעֲרָה תְּנַעֵר מִן / שְׂעָרָהּ עֲלֵי אֶרֶץ רְסִיסֶיהָ,
וְשׁוֹכְנִים כְּמוֹ חַיָּה אֲשֶׁר נָטְתָה / לְלִינָה וְחַצְרוֹתָם אֲבוּסֶיהָ,
וְכֻלָּם יְנוּסוּן מֵחֲתַת מָוֶת / כְּיוֹנָה אֲשֶׁר הַגֵּץ יְנִיסֶהָ,
וְסוֹפָם לְהִדַּמּוֹת לְצַלַּחַת / אֲשֶׁר שִׁבְּרוּ כָתִית חֲרָסֶיהָ.

שמואל הנגיד

DEATH
148

·24·

I contemplate the heaven and its stars,
      I see the things that swarm upon the ground,
And in my heart I know that they are made
      With skill, according to a well-made plan.
Pavillion-like the sky: just look aloft
      And see its curtains held with hooks and eyes;
The moon and stars are like a shepherd girl
      Who frees her sheep to graze upon a plain;
Against the clouds the moon appears to be
      A ship traversing oceans under sail;
The raincloud seems a girl, who walks along
      Her garden watering her myrtle plants;
The dew cloud's like a girl, tossing her head,
      Sprinkling sparkling droplets on the ground;
And those that dwell thereon are like a beast
      That lumbers toward the barn, their homes its stall.
They all are fleeing from the fear of death
      Like doves in terror of the eagle's claws.
In time they seem no better than a plate
      Broken and ground to dust—that is their fate.

Samuel the Nagid

DEATH

·24·

Like the preceding poem, this one starts with a tranquil description of natural phenomena associated with feelings of well-being and comfort, before turning into a dark meditation on death.

In the central portion of the poem, a line is devoted to each of several features of the natural world, comparing them with man-made things and human activities. The sky is a giant tent; the stars are silver hooks and eyes that hold its curtains firmly in place. Within this tent, the moon, other stars, rain clouds, and dew clouds are all in continuous, graceful motion.

Since the beginning of time, contemplation of the world's beauty has inspired man with feelings of awe and wonder. The idea that nature's grandeur and harmony imply a wise creator working by plan is only slightly less ancient. The poet counts on the reader's familiarity with these themes to lull him into a gentle, familiar feeling of order and peace. The similes of verses 4 to 7 also suggest grace, innocence, and loveliness.

All the natural phenomena take place within a closed, pro-tected environment, the tent-like sky. But this tent is the only thing that is fixed in place. Within it, all things are in motion. Already in the poem's first verse, the contents of the earth are called not crea-tures, things, or beings, but *remes,* "crawlers." The motions of the more remote entities are languid and undirected—sheep grazing in a meadow, a ship pushed gently by the breeze—whereas those closer to man engage in more energetic, purposeful activities—a girl watering plants or shaking raindrops from her hair.

Until this point, natural phenomena were compared to human beings and their activities. In verse 8, humans join the list of natu-ral phenomena as the subject of comparison to a lower rung on the continuum of life—the animal world.[1] The comparison is not in-tended to be flattering: The motion is the clumsy lumbering of dumb, weary beasts toward the satisfaction of brutish appetites and toward repose.

In verse 9, a third kind of motion is attributed to the earth's in-habitants: panic-stricken flight from the pursuit of death. The poet's seeing eye began by surveying the sky, then descended with pleasure toward earth; but now, abruptly, the eye jerks skyward again, this time to imagine death pursuing all those creatures whose graceful motions had seemed so delightful. Graceful or brutish, all motion inevitably spells dissolution. Even when external motion is lovely, the mind is made anxious by its knowledge of this motion's ultimate meaning.

The final motion violently reduces man and beast to the level of inanimate beings, or dust. By crowding the last verse with three different levels of inanimate existence, the author creates a poetic motion that far outstrips any of the earlier rhythms, producing a sense of tremendously rapid decay. Thus within the compass of a single hemistich, the plate (a useful, perhaps even lovely object) is turned first into shards (which are at least recognizable as remnants of the plate), and finally into undifferentiated, formless dust. Seeing that all things have returned to the dust of which they were made, we cannot help observing that the first item contemplated by the poet in verse 1, the sky, is actually called by a Hebrew word, the root of which means "to grind" or "to crush." In retrospect this choice of words appears as an intentional foreshadowing of the poem's theme.

·25·

$$--\cup\mid---\cup\mid---\cup\mid\mid-\cup\mid---\cup\mid---\cup$$

רְאֵה שֶׁמֶשׁ לְעֵת עֶרֶב אֲדֻמָּה / כְּאִלּוּ לָבְשָׁה תוֹלָע לְמִכְסָה,
תְּפַשֵּׁט פַּאֲתֵי צָפוֹן וְיָמִין / וְרוּחַ יָם בְּאַרְגָּמָן תְּכַסֶּה,
וְאֶרֶץ — עָזְבָה אוֹתָהּ עֲרֻמָּה / בְּצֵל הַלַּיְלָה תָּלִין וְתֶחְסֶה,
וְהַשַּׁחַק אֲזַי קָדַר, כְּאִלּוּ / בְּשַׂק עַל מוֹת יְקוּתִיאֵל מְכֻסֶּה.

שלמה אבן גבירול

·25·

Behold the sun at evening, red
    As if she wore vermillion robes.
Slipping the wraps from north and south
    She covers in purple the western side.
The earth—she leaves it cold and bare
    To huddle in shadows all night long.
At once the sky is dark; you'd think
    Sackcloth it wore for Yequtiel.

Solomon Ibn Gabirol

·25·

Upon the death of his patron, Yequtiel Ibn Ḥassan, Ibn Gabirol composed two poems: a formal eulogy of 102 verses and this little descriptive poem. To most Western tastes, the shorter far surpasses the longer in intensity.[1] It does not belong to the genre of eulogy; like the two preceding poems it is a charming nature description that turns dark at the end.

The poet watches the deepening colors of the evening sky. The brilliant color of the setting sun seems to be stolen from the earth, stripped like a red cape or blanket from its shoulders as the sun sinks into the western horizon. As the sun sets, the color deepens; and when at last the sky is dark the earth seems shrouded in sackcloth, mourning for Yequtiel.

The beauty of this poem derives not only from its imagery but also from the management of sounds. The first three verses in the Hebrew are dominated by the vowel *a*, which lends them a soft texture and a flowing line; the concentration of *k* sounds in verse 4 comes as a kind of explosion. This *k* derives from the name of Yequtiel himself, the man in whom Ibn Gabirol found not only a patron but also a protector. The name is kept in reserve until near the poem's end; only in the last hemistich do we discover the purpose of the visually lovely and phonically pleasing descriptive verses that came before.

‒‒◡|‒‒‒|‒|‒‒‒◡//‒‒◡|‒‒‒|‒‒‒

הֲלִינוֹתִי גְדוּד כָּבֵד בְּבִירָה / הֲרֵסוּהָ יְמֵי קֶדֶם קְצִינִים

וְיָשְׁנוּ עֲלֵי גַבָּהּ וְצִדָּהּ — / וְתַחְתֵּינוּ בְעָלֶיהָ יְשֵׁנִים.

וְדִבַּרְתִּי לְלִבִּי: אֵי קְהָלִים / וְעַמִּים שֶׁכְּנוּ בָזֹאת לְפָנִים?

וְאֵי בוֹנִים וּמַחֲרִיבִים וְשָׂרִים / וְדַלִּים וַעֲבָדִים וַאֲדוֹנִים?

וּמוֹלִידִים וְשַׁכּוּלִים וְאָבוֹת / וּבָנִים וַאֲבֵלִים וַחֲתָנִים?

וְעַם רַב נוֹלְדוּ אַחַר אֲחֵרִים / בְּיָמִים אַחֲרֵי יָמִים וְשָׁנִים

וְהָיוּ עַל פְּנֵי אֶרֶץ שְׁכֵנִים — / וְהֵם הַיּוֹם בְּלֵב אֶרֶץ שְׁכוּנִים,

וְקֶבֶר חָלְפוּ מֵאַרְמְנוֹתָם / וְעָפָר — מֵחֲצֵרִים נַעֲמָנִים,

וְאִלּוּ הֶעֱלוּ רֹאשָׁם וְיָצְאוּ — / שְׁלָלוּנוּ נְפָשִׁים וַעֲדָנִים.

אֱמֶת, נַפְשִׁי אֱמֶת כָּהֶם לְמָחָר / אֱהִי אֲנִי וְאֵלֶּה הֲהֲמוֹנִים!

שמואל הנגיד

I bade my troops encamp once at a town
  That enemies had razed in ancient times.
We pitched our tents and slept upon its site,
  While under us its former masters slept.
Then to myself I mused: "Where are the folk
  Who long ago inhabited this place?
Where are the men who built and those who wrecked?
  Where rich, where poor, where slaves, and where the
  lords?
Those who begot and those bereft, and sons
  And fathers, mourners, bridegrooms—where are they?
And generation after generation, born
  As centuries succeeded years of days.
Upon the face of earth they used to live,
  And yet today they lie within its heart.
They've changed their palaces for sepulchers;
  They've moved from lovely mansions into dirt.
But should they lift their heads and leave those graves,
  How easily they'd overwhelm our troops!"

Never forget, my soul, that one day soon
This mighty host and I will share their doom.

           Samuel the Nagid

This Ozymandias-like poem was written by the only Jew of the Middle Ages who could have written out of first-hand experience—the only known medieval Jew to command troops. Although Samuel's poems on death draw on the stock of international literary motifs shared by other Hebrew poets, they are sometimes stamped with the particular experiences of his own life.

Two verses at the beginning sketch the event that led the poet to these reflections, and one verse at the end states the moral to be drawn from them. The bulk of the poem follows the inner process of the poet's mind as he muses on the long history of the ghost town where his troops are encamped. These musings take the form of the familiar *ubi sunt* motif: Where, now, are the yearnings, loves, and sorrows of the past people of this town? The stress is not on the evanescence of mortal joys and sorrows, but on the great number and variety of people who once shared these feelings but now are gone. The question that opens the series of "where are . . ."'s in verse 3, literally means "Where are the communities and nations that once dwelled here?" Twelve of the thirteen words that make up verses 4 and 5 end in plural terminations, as do five of the nine words in verse 6. The effect of this repeated use of the plural may not be so evident in English, in which the plural is not always designated by a suffix ("Where rich, where poor . . .") and that suffix is but a single consonant. In Hebrew it is a whole syllable (*im* or *ot*). Most of the words in these verses end in *im,* and this termination is also part of the rhyme syllable (*nim*) at the end of every verse. Built into the single rhyme, and surging through the entire poem, is a feeling of multiplicity.

The poem is so affecting because it derives from a moment of power and pride in the speaker's life. He is the commander of an imposing troop of soldiers, camped on the ruin of a great city of old. He might consider himself, with satisfaction, a man who commands the living and the dead. But commanders have the habit of comparing the relative strength of troops; and even during a moment of mellow repose, this particular commander cannot keep his mind from moving in its habitual course. He considers even the most impossible eventualities: What if the dead of ages were to rise up as the enemy?

Commanders are also trained to make realistic appraisals, and this commander's knowledge that he would be vastly outnumbered by the army of the dead puts him in awe of his own puniness against the enormousness of the unseen forces around him, much as might the contemplation of the stars or other natural forces.[1] If even this mighty host has met its doom, what meaning is there in the exploits of the insignificant troop that has for the moment usurped its territory?—and what permanent value is there in the commander's own achievement?

This poem need not have arisen from an actual incident in the Nagid's military career, any more than the idea of Ozymandias came to Shelley through an actual encounter with a "traveller from an antique land." On the other hand, nothing could be more natural than that a man of the Nagid's background should adopt this form of expression. The commander's musings take place at night, when he is left alone contemplating the sleeping troops, like the poet at a wine party, awake after the other drinkers have drifted off, and thinking about the vanity of worldly pleasures. Thus both the military career and the social background of the poet provide the language for his meditation.

‎—‖—‖—‖—‖—‖—‖‖—‖—‖—‖—‖—‖—

‎עָבַרְתִּי עַל שׁוּק טַבָּחִים — / בּוֹ צֹאן וּשְׁוָרִים עַל יָדָם

‎וּמְרִיאִים רַב כִּדְגַת הַיָּם / וָעוֹף לָרֹב, בָּא יוֹם אֵידָם,

‎בּוֹ דָם קָפָא עַל גַּב דָּם, בּוֹ / שׁוֹחֲטִים רַבִּים יָרִיקוּ דָם.

‎וּלְצַדּוֹ צָדִים וּדְגַת יָם / כַּחוֹל, בִּכְלִי כָל אִישׁ צָדָם,

‎וּלְצַדָּם שׁוּק מַאֲפֶה — בַּיּוֹם / אוֹפֶה וּבְלַיְלָה לֹא רָדָם.

‎מִזֶּה אוֹפִים, מִזֶּה אוֹכְלִים, / מִזֶּה מוֹלִיכִים אֶת צֵידָם,

‎מִזֶּה נוֹשְׂאִים אֶל בָּתֵּיהֶם — / וַיָּכֶן לִבִּי אֶת סוֹדָם,

‎וָאֹמַר לָעוֹמְדִים: עַל מָה / כֹּה יִכְלוּ אֵלֶּה מְעוֹדָם?

‎מָה הֶבְדֵּל בֵּין אֵלֶּה לָכֶם, / בִּגְוִיעָתָם וּבְמוֹלָדָם

‎וּבְנוּמָתָם וּבְהָעִירָם / וּבְמוֹשָׁבָם וּבְמַעֲמָדָם?

‎לוּלֵי כִי צוּר הוּא הִטְעִימָם / לָכֶם, אָכֵן לֹא הִשְׁמִידָם,

‎אִלּוּ נָתַן בָּהֶם רוּחַ — / הֵם הֶאֱבִידוּ אֶת מַאֲבִידָם!

‎לָהֶם נֶפֶשׁ כָּכֶם גַּם לֵב, / כָּכֶם עַל אֶרֶץ לַהֲנִידָם,

‎לֹא נִמְצָא עֵת לֹא מֵת בּוֹ מֵת / אוֹ עֵת לֹא יוֹלִיד מוֹלִידָם.

‎לָזֹאת יָשִׂימוּ לֵב זַכִּים / וּנְסִיכִים גָּאוּ בִכְבוֹדָם:

‎אִם יָבִינוּ סוֹד הָעוֹלָם, / יֵדְעוּ כִּי זֶה כָל הָאָדָם!

‎שמואל הנגיד

DEATH
158

·27·

Passing a butchers' market once I watched
    The sheep and oxen standing side by side.
Cattle too many to count, like schools of fish,
    And flocks of fowl were all awaiting death.
Blood was congealing over clotted blood,
    While butchers, rank on rank, were spilling more.
Nearby was the fisher's market, filled with fish,
    And crowds of fishermen with hook and net;
Next was the bakers' market, where the ovens
    Burn all day and get no rest at night.

Men were baking, men were eating,
    Men were bearing home their kill;
Men were hawking beasts they'd hunted;
    I alone stood musing, still.

Then, speaking to the crowd I said,
                 "Why should
These beasts be snatched away from life to die?

How do they differ from you?

They die like you, like you are born;
They sleep like you, and wake at morn;
On haunches sit, on legs are borne.

Like you they have a soul, like you a will
To keep them wandering about the world.

To feed these beasts to you is God's design;
    If it were otherwise they'd not be dead.
If he restored their life—how easily
    They would destroy us, their destroyers, every one!
Was ever there a time when no one died,
    Or when begetting and begotten were forgot?"

This is a scene clear heads should keep in mind,
    Even princes, men who vaunt their state:
They've only to reflect on it to know
    That every living man will finish so.

Samuel the Nagid

DEATH

Like the preceding poem, to which it is a perfect companion piece, this one starts with the observation that the living are outnumbered by the dead. The scene is not a military camp but a market place: Consciousness of man's mortality is available to anyone who can walk the streets, not only to commanders of men.

Like all but a few of the poems in this book, this is a mono-rhymed poem, with all the lines of the same length and metrical pattern. But metrical uniformity does not necessarily mean rhythmical uniformity. Skillful use of internal rhymes and parallel syntactic patterns has enabled the poet to create blocks of verses contrasting in texture. The varied rhythmic and rhyming patterns in the translation are pale reflections of the great technical virtuosity of the original.

Here too, the poet's deliberate choice of rhyme syllable colors every line of the poem, for standing alone, the syllable *dam* is the Hebrew word for blood.[1] The butchers' market is no chrome-and-glass supermarket, with the meat neatly wrapped in plastic, but an Oriental bazaar, jam-packed with people and activity, color, motion, and blood. Live animals awaiting slaughter and carcasses of animals already turned into meat are side by side; blood is everywhere. The imminence of death lends the butchers' market a sordidness so intense that it spills over into the adjacent bakers' market, where, although no unpleasant activity is under way, the commotion of men, blindly pursuing the activities necessary to sustain human life, appears in a new and ugly light.

The poem's intensity is due partly to its stress on multiplicity and variety. We are impressed not only intellectually with the number of items observed in the bazaar, but also sensually; we *feel* their numerousness because of the poem's sound patterns. The rhyme syllable *dam* contains, in addition to the concept of blood, a grammatical element, the suffix *am*, which when attached to a noun becomes a plural possessive pronoun. Thus every line obsessively hammers out a subliminal message joining mortality and plurality. Other plural forms abound in the poem, for example in verses 6 and 7, where the plural termination *im* is repeated many times, confirmed by the rhyme syllable *am:*

mize of*im* mize okhl*im* meze molikh*im* et ṣed*am*
mize nos'*im* el bateh*em* vayaven libi et sod*am;*

In lines 9 and 10 we have a paroxysm of plural suffixes:

. . . bigvi'at*am* uvmolad*am*
uvnumat*am* uvha'ir*am* uvmoshav*am* uvama'mad*am.*

In building the poem around this effect, the poet ran a certain risk. His purpose was to make his listeners identify with the beasts in the butchers' market in order to know that they will meet the same fate. But the pronominal suffix contained in the word for blood is the *third* person pronoun, which could enable the auditor to distance himself from the throng of beasts and their doom. The ordinary bystander in the market place would be all too willing to think of death as the animals' fate, and to resist any inducement to reflect on his own; so too the reader. Yet the very words in which the speaker harangues the crowds about the similar destinies of men and animals provide for easy evasion: It is *their* life, *their* death, not mine.

But at the poem's end, through yet another linguistic resource, the poet closes this way out. The word for blood and the plural suffix meaning "their" are both contained in the Hebrew word for man, *adam;* by ending the poem with this word, the poet definitively yokes together the beasts in the bazaar, his readers, and all of mankind. There is no more space between them and us.

Of course all this had been said before. Ecclesiastes devoted several poignant verses to the idea, including a sentence that found its way into the liturgy: "Man has no superiority over beast, for all is vanity."[2] Ecclesiastes' book, however, concludes with an exhortation to piety: "The end of the matter, all having been heard: fear God, and keep his commandments; for this is the whole man."[3] It is this clause that provided the Nagid with the word *adam* as his final rhyme word. But when the poem ends with the words "this is all there is of man" it is referring *not* to the life of piety advocated by the epilogue of Ecclesiastes, but to the preceding lines of the poem and the word-picture of slaughtered beasts in the market place. The allusion to Ecclesiastes teases the classically educated reader by sidestepping the Preacher's message of consolation. "The whole of man" is not the observance of God's commandments, but the mortality that man shares with the ox.[4]

·28·

```
——∪|———∪|———∪//——∪|———∪|———∪
```

הֱקִיצוּנִי שְׂעִפַּי לַעֲבֹר עַל / מְלוֹן הוֹרַי וְכָל אַנְשֵׁי שְׁלוֹמִי.

שְׁאִלְתִּימוֹ — וְאֵין מַקְשִׁיב וּמֵשִׁיב: / הֲבָגְדוּ בִי עֲדֵי אָבִי וְאִמִּי?

בְּלִי לָשׁוֹן קְרָאוּנִי אֲלֵיהֶם / וְהֶרְאוּנִי לְצִדֵּיהֶם מְקוֹמִי.

משה אבן עזרא

·28·

I had the thought to pass the lodging where
  My parents and all my dearest friends abide.
I greeted them, but no one spoke. "Have Father
  And Mother both forgotten me?" I cried.
They heard. Without a word they summoned me,
  And pointed out my own place by their side.

Moses Ibn Ezra

DEATH
162

·28·

In the preceding poems the speaker was moved to reflect on the brevity of life by his observation of the works of nature or of man. The origin of the feeling that motivates this poem is more internal.

The speaker is driven to visit the cemetery. He does not call it a cemetery, but a lodging, literally, a "place to spend the night." The euphemism hints to us that his innermost being has not yet fully grasped the finality of his people's death. It is fully consistent with his attitude that he should attempt to address them, and should feel abandoned and angry when they fail to respond.

What happens to the speaker at the cemetery is a paradox. We think that we come to believe in our own mortality by experiencing the death of others close to us. This is only part of the speaker's experience. It is his sudden conviction of his own mortality that allows him to grasp the absolute finality of his parents' death. The two realizations resound infinitely against each other, becoming magnified each time. The beauty of the poem is that each time we reread it, now one, now the other of the two mortalities seems to claim priority as the starting point of the poet's meditation.

In death as in life, the speaker's parents prove wiser than he, wordlessly proclaiming from the grave their final piece of worldly wisdom. They seem to tell him that they are to be reunited. This is not meant as comfort. The speaker is not ready for comfort; his petulant cry in verse 2 reveals that he has not yet taken the prior step of grasping the reality of death itself.

Through the revelation that he will die, his parents' death becomes a reality for him. Read in this light, verse 3 does imply some small comfort. The speaker is not alone in having to leave life; at least we all lie together in the earth. More than the hope of inarticulate companionship, the dialogue with his parents cannot offer.

‒‒|‒‒‒|‒‒|‒‒∪||‒‒|‒|‒‒‒|‒‒‒∪

בְּשָׁנָה אוֹ שְׁנָתַיִם לְיֶלֶד / רְחִישָׁה יֵשׁ כְּצִפְעוֹנֵי נְחָשִׁים,

וּבֶן עֶשֶׂר יְקַפֵּץ בֵּין אֲבוֹתָיו / בְּאֶרֶץ כַּגְּדִי בֵּינוֹת תְּיָשִׁים.

וּבֶן עֶשְׂרִים אֲהוּב לַלֵּב וְאוֹהֵב / לְהִתְפָּאֵר וּמִתְהַדֵּר לְנָשִׁים,

וְיִתְנָאֶה וְיִתְגָּאֶה בְכֹחוֹ / וְשַׁחֲרוּתוֹ וְהוֹדוֹ בֶּן שְׁלֹשִׁים.

וְיִתַּמֵּם וְיִתְחַבֵּר בְּבוֹאוֹ / בְּאַרְבָּעִים לְרֵעָיו הַיְשִׁישִׁים—

וְיִיקַץ מִשְּׁנַת יַלְדוּת וְשַׁחֲרוּת / בִּלְבּוֹן רֹאשׁ וְזָקָן בֶּן חֲמִשִּׁים.

וּבַלְהוֹת הַזְּמָן עוֹבְרוֹת וְשָׁבוֹת / עֲלֵי אִישׁ עֵת אֲשֶׁר יָבוֹא בְשִׁשִּׁים.

וּמִשִּׁשִּׁים לְשִׁבְעִים נֶאֱנָח מִן / כְּאֵב זֹקֶן וְנִכְאֶה בֵּין קְדוֹשִׁים.

וְיִלְכֹּד הַזְּמָן אֶת בֶּן שְׁמוֹנִים, / בְּמַלְכֻּדְתּוֹ וּפָחָיו הַיְקוּשִׁים,

וְיִתְעָרְבוּ לְבֶן תִּשְׁעִים דְּרָכָיו / וְלֹא יֵדַע קְצִירִים מֶחֱרִישִׁים.

וּבֶן מֵאָה — וּמִי יִגַּע לְמֵאָה? — / לְתֶמַהּ יֵלְכוּ אֵלָיו אֲנָשִׁים,

וּבֶן מָוֶת — אָחִי תוֹלָע וְרָמָה / מָאוּס אַחִים מְגֹאָל הַלְּבוּשִׁים.

הֲלֹא אַחְבִּיר דְּבַר נֶהִי לְקוֹנֵן / לְבָבִי בוֹ וְגוּפִי לֶחֱדָשִׁים!

שמואל הנגיד

A child of one or two can get around
      By crawling like a snake upon the ground.
A ten-year old frolics in glee amid
      His elders, as among the goats the kid.
At twenty years a man's on pleasure bent;
      To captivate the girls his whole intent.
A man of thirty years is at his height;
      His looks, black hair, and strength are his delight.
When forty comes upon a man he tends
      To spend his time among his aging friends.
He puts his youthful daydreams out of sight,
      When fifty turns his hair and beard to white.
A man becomes obsessed with morbid fears
      On finding himself arrived at sixty years.
From sixty to seventy, groaning with age and gout,
      He sits among the elderly devout.
The eighty-year old man is scarce aware
      That Time has caught him in its mighty snare.
At ninety years a man lives in a daze;
      He can't tell plowing time from harvest days.
A hundred-year old man is but a freak;
      They come to stare at such a queer antique.
A corpse is something everybody loathes,
      With worms and maggots in its burial clothes.
And so laments and dirges I indite,
      To mourn my life and body day and night.

Samuel the Nagid

Commenting on the opening verse of Ecclesiastes—"'Vanity of vanities,' says the preacher, 'Vanity of vanities; all is vanity'"—an ancient rabbi said,

> A man sees seven worlds [in his lifetime]. A one-year-old is like a king borne in a litter, with everyone hugging and kissing him. A two- or three-year-old is like a pig, reaching out to muck. A ten-year-old prances like a kid. A twenty-year-old neighs like a horse, dresses up, and seeks a wife. Once he has a wife, he is like a donkey. When he has children he scrabbles shamelessly for bread like a dog. When he is old he is like a monkey.[1]

Our poem shares a few of its images with the Midrash, but drops the animal comparisons quite early in favor of a description of each of man's ages. The poem, as a result, sounds less like folklore, and more like a personal observation of life.

The repetition of the number sixty at the end of verse 7 and the beginning of verse 8 makes this age feel like a turning point, different from the others. This appears to be the age at which a man ceases to be an active participant in life, the first in which not man, but Time, is the active agent. A similar poem by Abraham Ibn Ezra makes the same point:

> Ask: where has the man of sixty gone?
> His trees no longer put forth twigs and roots,
> His sinews are thin and weak,
> No longer do they rise to fight his wars.[2]

— ‿ | — — ‿ | — ‿ / — ‿ / — ‿ | — ‿ | — — ‿

הֲתִהְיֶה בָךְ בְּבוֹא מָוֶת גְּבוּרָה / וְאִם מִיַּד שְׁאוֹל נַפְשְׁךָ שְׁמוּרָה?

מְעַט תֵּשֵׁב — וְיִקָּבְצוּ נְגִידִים / אֱלֵי בֵיתָךְ, כְּאִישׁ אֶחָד חֲבוּרָה,

וְתֻרְחַץ וְתֻנְקֶה וְתוּסַךְ / וְתֻמְשַׁךְ עֲלֵי אֶרֶץ כְּקוּרָה

וְתִלָּבֵשׁ בְּכָל תַּכְרִיךְ מְפֹאָר / וְתֻנַּח עֲלֵי מִטָּה כְעוּרָה,

וְתִשְׁמַע זַעֲקָה בַחֲדָרֶךָ / וְקוֹל צָרָה כְּמַבְכִּירָה מְצֵרָה.

וְיָקוּם אִישׁ לְבַכּוֹת אוֹהֲבֶיךָ / בְּהוֹלִיכָם לְךָ אֶל הַקְּבוּרָה,

וְיָקוּמוּ עֲלֵי קִבְרְךָ הֲמוֹנִים / וְתֻנְתַּן בְּתוֹךְ שׁוּחָה חֲפוּרָה,

וְיָשׁוּבוּ חֲפוּיֵי רֹאשׁ וְעֵינָם / כְּמוֹ נַחַל וּבִלְבָבָם מְדוּרָה —

וְיַשְׁכִּימוּ לְחַלֵּק אֶת רְכוּשָׁךְ / וְיֵהָפֵךְ נְהִי פִּיהֶם לְשִׁירָה.

בְּכֵה נַפְשְׁךָ בְּעוֹדָךְ חַי וְחִיל יוֹם / פְּקֻדָּתָךְ יְרָא, לִבִּי, וְגוּרָה!

שמואל הנגיד

·30·

Will you have strength to fight when death arrives?
      Are you exempted somehow from the grave?
Just wait a while: soon some gentlemen
      Will form a little party at your house.
They'll wash you, clean you, rub you with perfume,
      And set you like a plank upon the ground.
They'll dress you up in all the finest shrouds,
      And lay you out upon the hated bed.
And then a cry will sound throughout your rooms,
      A cry of pain, like women in travail.
One man will lead your loved ones in lament,
      While others drag you out to be interred.
A crowd will stand around your grave and watch
      You being laid inside the deep-dug pit.
And then they'll turn toward home, their hair undone,
      Their eyes like rivers and their hearts aflame.
But when next day they rise to share your wealth,
      The moans in their very mouths will turn to song.
Bewail yourself, my heart, while you are here,
      And of your day of death, live, heart, in fear.

Samuel the Nagid

DEATH
169

·30·

This poem seems to have been written for the sheer pleasure of its macabre fantasy of death. The moral tacked on at the end reads like an afterthought, a pious justification of the poet's self-indulgence.

The last line is not even that pious. It does not exhort to repentance any more than it recommends eating, drinking, and merrymaking. It tells the reader only to weep and fear, two activities that are static in themselves. It tells the reader how to *feel*, not how to *act*. We know this poem to be a secular one because it is from a secular collection, *Ben Qohelet* by Samuel the Nagid. But even if we did not know its provenance, we could identify it as a secular poem on purely internal literary grounds.

The macabre fantasy is far less extreme than Poe's loving depictions of worms and rotting flesh. This poet is fascinated more with the social aspects of dying. He dwells on the alteration in social status of a man turned corpse. It is clear from the beginning that the speaker is a dignitary of some kind, a man of valor (*gevura*, here translated "strength"), used to enjoying special exemptions.[1] Neither of these can withstand death. His mourners are dignitaries—*negidim*, here translated as "gentlemen." The exact application of this honorific is disputed, but it was never applied to any but the most outstanding public figures, men like Samuel himself. The shape of the poem indicates the transition from the active, worldly life led by such a man to the passive existence that follows. The activity of worms is not within the poem's scope.

The part of speech best suited for depicting the active life is the verb, and to be sure, four of them are crowded into verse 3, all predicated on the corpse. Since he is dead, they are of necessity in the passive voice; but even so, they charge the dead man's environment with activity, in an ironic imitation of the hectic atmosphere that surrounded him in life. But little by little the activity diminishes. In verse 4 the number of verbs is reduced to two, still predicated on the corpse, and still passive. Verse 5 has only one verb, also passive. Owing to a peculiarity of Hebrew morphology, its form is identical with that of the preceding verbs, though its agent is no longer the corpse but the cry raised by the mourners. This verb is a pivot on which the action turns away from the corpse. Verses 6 through 9 all begin with active verbs predicated of the mourners. At first their activity concerns the deceased, as they weep and lament; but by verse 9 they are concerned only with his property, which they distribute among themselves. Since their laments are thus destined to turn to song, the only true lament is that which a man makes for himself.

‏‒‒◡‖‒‒‒┃‒◡‖‒◡╱╱‒‒╱┃‒‒‒┃‒◡

‏וְלֵב נָבוּב וְתוּשִׁיָּה סְתוּמָה / וְגוּף נִרְאֶה וְנֶפֶשׁ נַעֲלָמָה,

‏וְאֶרֶץ שׁוֹחֲרֶיהָ יִמְצְאוּ רַע / וְלֹא שָׂשׂוֹן לְאָדָם בָּאֲדָמָה:

‏וְעֶבֶד יַהֲרֹג הַיּוֹם אֲדוֹנָיו, / וְשִׁפְחָה יִסְּרָה מַלְכָּהּ, וְאָמָּה,

‏וּבֵן יָקוּם עֲלֵי אָבִיו וְאִמּוֹ / וְכֵן הַבַּת בְּאָבִיהָ וְאִמָּהּ.

‏יְדִידִי, רָאֲתָה עֵינִי בְּחֶבֶל, / אֲשֶׁר הַטּוֹב בְּעֵינֵי כֹל — מְהוּמָה!

‏יְמֵי חַיֵּי אֱנוֹשׁ יִשָּׂא עֲמָלִים / וְיִשָּׂא אַחֲרִיתוֹ גּוּשׁ וְרִמָּה.

‏וְתָשׁוּב הָאֲדָמָה לָאֲדָמָה / וְתַעַל הַנְּשָׁמָה לַנְּשָׁמָה.

‏שלמה אבן גבירול

·31·

The mind is flawed, the way to wisdom blocked;
 The body alone is seen, the soul is hid,
And those who seek the world find only ill;
 A man can get no pleasure here on earth.
The servant rises up and kills his lord,
 And serving girls attack their mistresses.
Sons are raising hands against their parents,
 Daughters too oppose their parents' will.
My friend, from what I've seen of life I'd say
 The best that one can hope is to go mad.
However long you live you suffer toil,
 And in the end you suffer rot and worms.
Then finally the clay goes back to clay;
 At last the soul ascends to join the Soul.

Solomon Ibn Gabirol

The only truly depressing poem in this anthology is also the only one that refuses to concede anything to the pleasures of life. It has been selected mainly for the sake of contrast, setting off the other poems on death to show how strong their hold on life really is. The darkest of the other poems on death merely laments the passing of earthly joys; this poem denies their reality.

The work of a man who was a pessimist on philosophical grounds, this poem is founded on the common notion that the body is a kind of prison in which the soul is entrapped and from which it continually yearns to escape. The individual soul is but a fragment of a larger, universal soul, which it can rejoin only upon the dissolution of the body, as in verse 10. From this perspective, the life of the flesh is at best banal; at worst, it has the power to distract the soul from ultimate realities, corrupting its purity and preventing its union with the world-soul.

It is not hard to see how this way of looking at life could be integrated with religious doctrine; there is some precedent in the sayings of the ancient rabbis and the old synagogue poetry.[1] But the present poem does not derive from the religious tradition, nor does it exhort to any particular conduct. It is a secular meditation on the meaninglessness of life, which states plainly that death is to be preferred.

Consistent with its premise that the body is worthless, this poem does not lament the transience of life and its pleasures. Its main theme and symbol is the upsetting of the social hierarchy, servants usurping the place of their masters and children rebelling against their parents. In reading this poem it is important to resist the temptation to look for some event in the social history of medieval Spain or in Ibn Gabirol's biography as the motivation for his complaint.

It is customary to infer from Ibn Gabirol's poems that he passed his short life in bitterness over his frustrated social aspirations and the lack of understanding with which his ideas and poetry were received. This is true, as far as it goes. His bitterness often takes the form of complaint about the social indignities he suffered, especially in Saragossa, after the death of his patron Yequtiel Ibn Hassan:

> Considered a stranger, an outsider,
>   Living where the ostriches dwell,
> Surrounded by cheats and fools,
>   Though he is wise as Tahkemoni,[2]
> . . . .
> By a people whose ancestors were too low
>   To be sheep dogs for my flocks.[3]

Though Ibn Gabirol's failure to achieve the recognition he desired may very well underlie the poem's imagery, focusing attention on his biography means turning away from the poem's inner logic. Ibn Gabirol's complaint about life at large is symbolized by precisely the social outrages described in verses 3 and 4. The overthrow of the social hierarchy mirrors the reversal of the cosmic hierarchy in the minds of the Philistine masses, who think only of the life of the body, and for whom the life of the soul is as nothing. In fact, Ibn Gabirol's attitude in this poem, as in some others, is the opposite of the *carpe diem* principle: not "seize the day" for pleasure or repentance, as the sensualists and the pietists advise, but "waste the day," i.e., get through it as quickly as possible so that real life can begin.

Afterword

The poem by Ibn Gabirol that ends this anthology points the way out of the Golden Age. Ibn Gabirol lived on the margin of a brilliant culture and longed to be included in courtly life; yet at the same time he loathed it from the core of his being for its materialism and shallow conventionality. Halevi, a much more stable personality and far better integrated in the culture, eventually chose to unravel his tangled loyalties by devoting himself to a purer and more austere set of ideals. Conventional piety did not satisfy these men, the one profoundly intellectual, and the other profoundly Jewish.

But the Golden Age style in poetry and life did not end because of these defections. When in the course of the twelfth century the Jewish leadership relocated in the Christian courts of Castile, Navarre, and Aragon, a new generation of Arabic-speaking courtier-rabbis arose, and the poetic tradition soon revived. The new circumstances added novel cultural elements to the already complex intellectual life of the courtier-rabbis. Increased contact with the Christian world and the nascent Romance literatures; the new status of the Jews as teachers of high Arabic culture to the less sophisti-

177

cated Christian world; new intellectual movements such as mysticism and Aristotelianism; and the eventual decline of toleration on the part of the host people—all these brought about changes in the secular writing of the Jews that make it expedient to separate this period from the Golden Age, despite the similarities between them.

The defection of two of the Golden Age's greatest talents is not as stunning a critique of the culture as it might appear. Dramatic as was Halevi's gesture in leaving Spain, he lived his last months among the Jews of Egypt in exactly the same manner as he had lived among his Andalusian brethren—whether from choice or necessity we shall probably never know. Ibn Gabirol's philosophical principles and psychological predisposition made him unsuited for any human society.

There is much to admire in the courtier-rabbis' attempt to remain loyal to Judaism while enjoying to the full the attractions of Arabic culture. The synthesis was at least fruitful. We know that some members of the Jewish upper class abandoned their Jewish ties altogether, and we may assume that others retreated from the challenge of Arabic culture into a defensive Judaism. It is certain that the lives of both these groups were the poorer for their choice.

Notes

INTRODUCTION

1. Abraham Ibn Daud, *Sefer ha-Qabbalah: The Book of Tradition,* ed. and trans. G. D. Cohen (Philadelphia: The Jewish Publication Society of America, 1967), p. 102; Hebrew text, p. 73.

2. Introductions to the history and culture of the Jews in Muslim Spain are listed at the end of this book, under the heading *For Further Reading.*

3. J. Weiss, *"Tarbut ḥaṣranit veshira ḥaṣranit," Kinnus lemad͑e hayahadut* 1 (1952): 396–403; D. Pagis, *Shirat haḥol vetorat hashir lemoshe ibn ezra uvene doro* (Jerusalem: Mosad Bialik, 1970), p. 257.

4. Ḥ. Schirmann, *Hashira ha͑ivrit besefarad uveprovans* (Jerusalem and Tel Aviv: Bialik Institute and Dvir Publishing Co., 1954), 1:223–225; the translation by Frederick P. Bargebuhr in *The Alhambra: A Cycle of Studies on the Eleventh Century in Moorish Spain* (Berlin: Walter de Gruyter and Co., 1968), pp. 97–101 is learned, but tendentious.

5. Josh. 10:12. The Hebrew verb used by both Joshua and Ibn Gabirol to make the sun halt in its course ordinarily means "to be silent."

6. I have studied this feature of Arabic versification systematically in my book *Form and Structure in the Poetry of al-Mu͑tamid Ibn ͑Abbad* (Leiden: E. J. Brill, 1975).

7. P. Cachia in W. M. Watt, *A History of Islamic Spain* (Edinburgh: University Press, 1965), p. 72.

8. By Solomon Ibn Gabirol. Hebrew text in Schirmann, *Hashira ha͑ivrit,* 1:219; with English translation differing somewhat from mine, in T. Carmi, *The Penguin Book of Hebrew Verse* (New York: Penguin Books, 1981), p. 310; discussed in Bargebuhr, *The Alhambra,* pp. 335, 339. My translation of *ḥameda et pene* as "longed to" differs from previous interpretations, but is justified by the context and

179

by other usages of the word. My point about reciprocity would not be vitiated by the usual interpretation, "envied."

9. Sources in my *Form and Structure*. The passage is quoted in a similar connection by H. Pérès, *La poésie andalouse en arabe classique au xi⁰ siècle*, 2nd ed. (Paris: Librairie d'amérique et d'orient Adrien-Maisonneuve, 1953), p. 62.

10. Ḥ. Brody, *Moshe ibn ezra: shire hahol* (Berlin: Schocken Press, 1935), 1:5. Other examples in Shraga Abramson, *Bileshon qodmim: mehqar beshirat yisrael besefarad* (Jerusalem: Schocken Institute for Jewish Research of the Jewish Theological Seminary of America, 1965), p. 43.

11. Five treatises are listed and described in D. Pagis, *Shirat hahol vetorat hashir*, pp. 12–13 and 16–17. Only the *Kitab al-muhadara wa'l-mudhakara* has been published; three other works are lost. Of the two surviving, neither has been translated into English.

12. The system is thoroughly explained in the article "Prosody, Hebrew" by B. Hrushovsky, *Encyclopaedia Judaica* (Jerusalem: Keter Publishing House Ltd., 1972), 13:1211–1220.

13. The similarity of the *muwashshah* to certain forms of troubadour poetry and the Romance content of the *kharajāt* have aroused great interest among Western scholars. Though no longer the last word on the subject, S. M. Stern's book, *Hispano-Arabic Strophic Poetry*, ed. L. P. Harvey (Oxford: Clarendon Press, 1974) may be profitably consulted by the serious student. A brave attempt to capture the "sting" effect of the *kharja* is an English imitation of a *muwashashah* in H. A. R. Gibb, *Arabic Literature: An Introduction* (Oxford: Clarendon Press, 1963), pp. 111–112. See also J. T. Monroe, *Hispano-Arabic Poetry: A Student Anthology* (Berkeley: University of California Press, 1974), pp. 28–33.

1 WINE

Introduction

1. In the translations and discussions I have permitted myself the use of this Arabic word, which may be known to English readers through Edward Fitzgerald's *Rubáiyát of Omar Khayyám*.

2. Quoted and discussed by A. Hamori, *On the Art of Medieval Arabic Literature* (Princeton: Princeton University Press, 1974), pp. 55–56. On the poet, see later, n. 14.

3. *Rubáiyát of Omar Khayyám the Astronomer-Poet of Persia*, trans. E. Fitzgerald (New York: Books, Inc., n.d.), p. 113. This edition contains all five versions of Fitzgerald's work; the quotation is from the fourth edition, dated 1879.

4. Pérès, *La poésie andalouse*, pp. 371–393.

5. He mentions specifically "poems in praise of valor and generosity . . . or in praise of wine . . . Hebrew *muwashshahat*." Commentary on the Mishna, *Avot* 1.16 in *Mishna ⁽im perush rabbenu moshe ben maimon: seder neziqin*, ed. J. Kafah (Jerusalem: Mossad Harav Kook, 1964), p. 419.

6. Pérès, *La poésie andalouse*, p. 377.

7. The conversation at a soirée that might have taken place in the home of an early twelfth-century courtier-rabbi has been imaginatively constructed out of historical sources by G. D. Cohen in his edition of Abraham Ibn Daud's *Sefer ha-Qabbalah: The Book of Tradition*, pp. xxi–xxii.

8. Ḥ. Schirmann, *"Ḥaye yehuda halevi,"* *Tarbiz* 9 (1938): 38–39; S. Abramson, *"Iggeret rav yehuda halevi lerav moshe ibn ezra"* in *Sefer Ḥayim Schirmann* (Jerusalem: Schocken Institute for Jewish Research, 1970), pp. 397–411.

9. Judah al-Ḥarizi, *Taḥkemoni,* ed. Y. Toporowski (Jerusalem: *Maḥbarot lesifrut,* 1952), pp. 263–265; see also the English translation in the two-volume work by V. E. Reichert (Jerusalem: R. H. Cohen's Press, 1965–1973), 2:171–186. My own translation takes a few liberties with the meaning in order to suggest the style of the original, which is the main point in passages such as this.

10. Al-Ḥarizi, *Taḥkemoni,* pp. 275–281; Reichert, 2:187–196. I concede my inability to translate even one such poem into English.

11. Al-Ḥarizi, *Taḥkemoni,* pp. 240–241; Reichert, 2:136–142.

12. Translation by J. T. Monroe in his *Hispano-Arabic Poetry,* pp. 260–261. The deliciously obscene continuation of the poem is omitted here so as not to divert attention from the main point.

13. See the introduction to Chapter II, later.

14. See E. Wagner, *Abu Nuwas: Eine Studie zur arabischen Literatur der frühen Abbasidenzeit* (Wiesbaden, Franz Steiner Verlag, 1965).

15. The *ʿAnaq* was published by H. Brody in *Moshe ibn ezra: shire haḥol,* 1:297–404, with a commentary in vol. 3 (Jerusalem: Schocken Institute, 1978), pp. 37–153. The motif-index to the poems of Moses Ibn Ezra in vol. 3, pp. 313–315, compiled by D. Pagis, although based on the works of a single poet, is a useful guide to Hebrew wine poetry as a whole.

16. Brody, *Moshe ibn ezra,* 1:157. *Dīwān* is the Arabic word, used also by Hebrew poets, for a collection of poems.

17. The wine poems, which are scattered throughout the first part of the Nagid's *diwan,* were collected into a single corpus by D. Jarden in his *Diwan shemuel hanagid: ben tehilim* (Jerusalem: Hebrew Union College Press, 1966), pp. 279–295.

18. For a discussion of the genre, see the literature cited by F. Krenkow and G. LeComte in the article *"Ḳaṣīda," Encyclopedia of Islam²* (Leiden: E. J. Brill, 1976), 2:713–714.

19. A translation of his masterpiece is found in *Selected Poems of Moses Ibn Ezra,* trans. S. Solis-Cohen, ed. H. Brody (Philadelphia: The Jewish Publication Society of America, 1945), pp. 16–22.

20. On the prohibition of wine, see *Quran* 5:92 and I. Goldziher, *Introduction to Islamic Theology and Law,* trans. A. Hamori and R. Hamori (Princeton: Princeton University Press, 1981), pp. 59–63; on the prohibition of music, see H. G. Farmer, *A History of Arabian Music to the XIIth Century* (London: Luzac & Co., Ltd., 1929), pp. 20–38. On music in Judaism, see B. Cohen, *The Responsum of Maimonides Concerning Music* (New York, 1935); Salo Wittmayer Baron, *A Social and Religious History of the Jews²* (New York: Columbia University Press, 1958), 7:203–206 and the accompanying notes; and, especially, H. G. Farmer, *Maimonides on Listening to Music* (Hertford, England, 1941).

21. Translated by A. Hamori in the insightful chapter entitled "The Poet as Ritual Clown" in his *On the Art of Medieval Arabic Literature,* p. 52.

22. I. Goldziher, *Muslim Studies,* ed. S. M. Stern, trans. C. R. Barber and S. M. Stern (London: George Allen and Unwin, Ltd., 1967) 1:11–44; G. E. von Grunebaum, *Medieval Islam: A Study in Cultural Orientation²* (Chicago: The University of Chicago Press, 1953), p. 121.

23. Ibn Khaldun, *The Muqaddimah: An Introduction to History²* (London: Routledge and Kegan Paul, 1967), 3:300–305.

24. Pérès, *La poésie andalouse,* p. 28.

NOTES

25. Baron, *Social and Religious History* 5 : 185, 257–258, 271.

26. On accepting exile in the right spirit, see Judah Halevi, *Kitab al Khazari,* trans. H. Hirschfeld with a preface by M. M. Kaplan (New York: Bernard G. Richards Co., Inc., 1927), pp. 79–80 (Part I, paragraph 115).

27. Ps. 106 : 35; applied to acculturation by Moshe Ibn Ezra, *Kitab al-muḥaḍara waʾl-mudhakara,* ed. A. S. Halkin (Jerusalem: Sumptibus Societatis Mekize Nirdamim, 1975), p. 48. The first word of the verse, *vayitʿarevu,* could mean "they mingled" or "they became Arabized," a *double entendre* that could not have been missed by Ibn Ezra's readers.

28. See my "Rabbi Moshe Ibn Ezra on the Legitimacy of Poetry," *Medievalia et Humanistica* N.S. 7 (1976): 101–115.

29. A vividly imagined reconstruction of such a situation is found in E. Ashtor, *Qorot hayehudim bisefarad hamuslimit* I (Jerusalem, Kiryat Sepher Ltd., 1960), 1 : 126–127. This memorable passage was unfortunately—and tacitly—omitted from the English translation of the book.

30. From a responsum by Hai Gaon published by B. M. Lewin in *"Teshuvot rav haya gaon leqairawan,"* *Ginze Qedem* 5 (1933): 58–59.

Poem 1

Source:

Schirmann, *Hashira haʿivrit,* 1 : 371.

Translations:

N. Kozodoy, "Reading Medieval Hebrew Love Poetry," *AJS Review* 2 (1977): 121.

Solis-Cohen and Brody, *Selected Poems,* p. 45.

Carmi, *Penguin Book,* p. 323.

Discussion:

Kozodoy, *ibid.,* pp. 121–126.

D. Pagis, *Ḥiddush umasoret beshirat haḥol* (Jerusalem: Keter Publishing House Ltd., 1976), pp. 265–66.

1. II Sam. 23 : 1.

2. II Kings 25 : 29.

3. Gen. 41 : 14, 39–43.

4. Gen. 37 : 3, II Sam. 13 : 18.

5. Num. 9 : 13.

6. F. Brown, et al., *A Hebrew and English Lexicon of the Old Testament* (Oxford: Clarendon Press, 1907), p. 308a, s.v. *ḥetʾ.*

7. The word *akh,* which opens verse 4, and which, as noted previously, is especially stressed, has a legalistic tone that could not be missed by Hebraists steeped in the tradition of rabbinic exegesis.

Poem 2

Source:

Schirmann, *Hashira haʿivrit,* 1 : 34. The text of line 2 has been corrected in accordance with E. Fleischer, *"Ḥiqre shira ufiyyut,"* *Tarbiz* 39 (1969–1970): 33–35.

Translations:

D. Goldstein, *Hebrew Poems from Spain* (New York: Schocken Books, 1966), pp. 15–16.

Carmi, *Penguin Book*, p. 280.

Bargebuhr, *The Alhambra*, pp. 56–57.

Discussion:

Y. Levin, *Shemuel hannagid* (Tel Aviv: Hakibbutz Hameuchad, 1962–1963), pp. 17–18.

Bargebuhr, *ibid.*

1. H. Brody, *Diwan des Abu-l-Ḥasan Jehuda ha-Levi*, (Berlin: M'kize Nirdamim, . 1909), 2:222.

2. Schirmann, *Hashira haᶜivrit*, 1:34.

Poem 3

Source:

Schirmann, *Hashira haᶜivrit*, 1:161–162.

Translations:

Carmi, *Penguin Book*, p. 296.

L. J. Weinberger, *Jewish Prince in Moslem Spain: Selected Poems of Samuel Ibn Nagrela* (University, Alabama: University of Alabama Press, 1973), p. 114.

Discussion:

D. Pagis, "'And Drink Thy Wine With Joy': Hedonistic Speculation in Three Wine Songs by Samuel Hannagid" (Hebrew), in *Studies in Literature Presented to Simon Halkin*, ed. E. Fleischer (Jerusalem: Magnes Press, 1973), pp. 133–140.

1. Noted by S. Abramson in his edition of *Ben qohelet* by Samuel the Nagid (Tel Aviv: *Mahbarot lesifrut*, 1952–1953), p. 185.

2. Pesaḥim 68b, Beṣa 15b. The debate hinges on the word *lakhem* (to you), which is also the last word of verse 2b of our poem.

3. This tone is definitely struck in a famous poem of self-justification by the Nagid (Schirmann, *Hashira haᶜivrit*, 1:109–111, verses 43–44; translated by Weinberger, *Jewish Prince*, pp. 50–52) and in his little prayer in time of battle (Schirmann, *Hashira haᶜivrit*, 1:93; translation in Carmi, *Penguin Book*, p. 288).

Poem 4

Source:

Schirmann, *Hashira haᶜivrit*, 1:164.

Translations:

Weinberger, *Jewish Prince*, p. 112.

Discussion:

1. I am not aware of any publications dealing with this aspect of medieval Hebrew versification, but my book *Form and Structure* deals at length with the phenomenon in Arabic poetry.

2. I have discussed this practice in Arabic poetry in *Form and Structure*, pp. 36–59.

Poem 5

Source:

Schirmann, *Hashira haᶜivrit*, 1:157.

Translations:

Weinberger, *Jewish Prince*, p. 100–101.

NOTES
183

Discussion:

Pagis, "'And Drink Thy Wine With Joy,'" pp. 140–148.

1. Eccles. 3:19–20, especially as cited by the Babylonian Talmud, Ḥagiga 13a. Numerous citations have been collected by M. S. Segal in *Sefer ben sira hashalem*[2] (Jerusalem: Bialik Foundation, 1971–1972), p. 17, in his comment on the passage.

2. The same kind of false opening in the style of a poem on asceticism by Abu Nuwas is discussed by Hamori, *On the Art of Medieval Arabic Literature*, p. 51.

3. Wagner, *Abu Nuwas*, pp. 304–305.

4. Many examples have been cited by D. Yellin, *Torat hashira hasefaradit*[2] (Jerusalem: Magnes Press, 1973), pp. 102–117.

5. I Chron. 25:1–8.

6. Examples are everywhere in his poetry. See his *Diwan*, ed. Jarden, pp. 33–34.

7. Jarden, *Diwan*, p. 33 (poem 7, verse 38).

8. Other commentators have suggested Eccles. 8:8, 9:7, and 12:13. Pagis also accepts 11:9, but with a different interpretation.

9. The sources, listed by L. Ginzberg, *The Legends of the Jews* (Philadelphia: The Jewish Publication Society of America, 1913–1938), 5:29, n. 79, include the Aramaic paraphrase of Eccles. 9:7, which is alluded to in verse 10 of the poem. The banquet is particularly associated with David; see Ginzberg, *ibid.*, 4:114–116.

10. This is Pagis' interpretation, based on Jerusalem Talmud Qiddushin 66b; Babylonian Talmud Nedarim 10b.

Poem 6

Source:

Schirmann, *Hashira haʿivrit*, 1:165.

Translations:

Weinberger, *Jewish Prince*, p. 111.

Discussion:

Bargebuhr, *The Alhambra*, pp. 357–358.

1. The Hebrew participle *mashqe*, used in verse 3 with verbal force, is a cognate of the Arabic word *sāqī*, or *sáki*, as spelled by Fitzgerald.

Poem 7

Source:

Schirmann, *Hashira haʿivrit*, 1:373.

1. John Keats, "Ode to Melancholy," in John Keats and Percy Bysshe Shelley, *Complete Poetical Works* (New York: The Modern Library, n.d.), p. 194.

2. II Kings 3:15. Literally translated, the last hemistich of the poem reads: "Revive me when the minstrel plays."

3. Moses Ibn Ezra, *Kitab al-muḥaḍara*, pp. 22–27; in the Hebrew translation by B.-Z. Halper (Leipzig: Stiebel, 1924), pp. 44–46. See also my "Rabbi Moshe Ibn Ezra on the Legitimacy of Poetry."

4. M. Guadefroy-Demombynes, introduction to *Ibn Qotaïba: Introduction au livre de la poésie et des poètes* (Paris: Société d'édition "Les Belles Lettres," 1947), p. xli.

5. From his poem beginning ʿad an begalut shuleḥu shaloaḥ. Solis-Cohen and Brody, *Selected Poems*, pp. 2–5 (lines 41–42 of the poem).

Poem 8

Source:
Schirmann, *Hashira haʿivrit,* 1 : 168.
Translations:
Weinberger, *Jewish Prince,* p. 106.
Carmi, *Penguin Book,* p. 298.
 1. Carmi resorted to the same device in his translation.
 2. *Midrash Bereshit Rabba,*² ed. J. Theodor and Ch. Albeck (Jerusalem: Wahrmann Books, 1965), p. 109 (Chapter 13, paragraph 10).
 3. See, for example, section 27 of Ibn Gabirol's philosophical poem *Keter Malkhut* in I. Zangwill and I. Davidson, *Selected Religious Poems of Solomon Ibn Gabirol* (Philadelphia: The Jewish Publication Society of America, 1924), pp. 102−103.

Poem 9

Source:
Schirmann, *Hashira haʿivrit,* 1 : 166.
Translation:
Weinberger, *Jewish Prince,* p. 109.
 1. See, for example, E. W. Lane, *An Arabic-English Lexicon* (London: Williams and Nargate, 1863−1893), 4 : 1600a, s.v. *shaml.*

Poem 10

Source:
Schirmann, *Hashira haʿivrit,* 1 : 167.
Translation:
Weinberger, *Jewish Prince,* p. 108.
 1. Exod. 9 : 24, as interpreted in Shemot Rabba 12 : 4.

2 WOMEN

Introduction

 1. ʿAli Ibn Ḥazm, *The Ring of the Dove,* trans. A. J. Arberry (London: Luzac & Company, Ltd., 1953); *A Book Containing the Risala Known as the Dove's Neck-Ring about Love and Lovers,* trans. A. R. Nykl (Paris: Paul Geuther, 1931).
 2. The poem is anthologized in Monroe, *Hispano-Arabic Poetry,* pp. 178−187. The story of Ibn Zaidun and Wallada is told in A. R. Nykl, *Hispano-Arabic Poetry and its Relations with the Old Provençal Troubadours* (Baltimore, 1946), pp. 106−121, including translations of many of the poems exchanged by the lovers.
 3. The story and a few poems are given in Nykl, *Hispano-Arabic Poetry,* pp. 134−154.
 4. Monroe, *Hispano-Arabic Poetry,* p. 19; S. Lug, *Poetic Techniques and Conceptual Elements in Ibn Zaidun's Love Poetry* (Washington, D.C.: University Press of America, 1982), pp. 133−160.
 5. For a survey of this literature, including some remarkable statistics, see

NOTES
185

S. Spiegel, "On Medieval Hebrew Poetry" in *The Jews: Their History, Culture, and Religion*³ (Philadelphia: The Jewish Publication Society of America, 1960), 1:854–892.

6. The word *ghazal* is sometimes used to designate the kind of poem here described and sometimes to designate the themes of love poetry even when couched in other forms. I restrict my usage to the former for the sake of clarity.

7. I am aware of only one long *ghazal* poem in Hebrew. See Judah Halevi, *Diwan*, ed. Brody, 2:7–10.

8. Some of the remarks in the following pages are drawn, with revision, from my as yet unpublished paper, written in 1978, entitled "Courtly Love in the Hebrew Tradition." These two categories do not classify all love poems; for a poem not belonging to either category, see poem 14.

9. On the troubadours' practice of protecting the beloved by not revealing her name, see A. Bonner, *Songs of the Troubadours* (New York: Schocken Books, 1972), p. 23; for Andalusian Arabs, see Ibn Ḥazm, *The Ring of the Dove*, p. 79 and contrast with p. 86. Various words for deer are used in the Song of Songs and Proverbs as figures of speech connected with lovers; they are very common in Arabic poetry and are found in Greek and medieval Latin. See K. J. Dover, *Greek Homosexuality* (New York: Vintage Books, 1980), p. 87; E. R. Curtius, *European Literature and the Latin Middle Ages*, trans. W. R. Trask (New York: Harper & Row, 1953), p. 115.

10. For clarity I generally refer to the lover in the masculine gender and the beloved in the feminine gender.

11. Brody, *Moshe ibn ezra*, 1:185–188.

12. See F. Rosenthal, "Fiction and Reality: Sources for the Role of Sex in Medieval Muslim Society" in *Society and the Sexes in Medieval Islam*, ed. A. L. al-Sayyid-Marsot (Malibu, California: Udena Publications, 1979), pp. 3–22. For the same dichotomy in medieval Christendom, see A. J. Denomy, *The Heresy of Courtly Love* (New York: The Declan X. McMullen Co., Inc., 1947), p. 28; Curtius, *European Literature*, pp. 116–117.

13. For a definitive statement on this topic, see S. D. Goitein, "The Sexual Mores of the Common People," in *Society and the Sexes in Medieval Islam*, ed. al-Sayyid-Marsot, pp. 43–61. On the inconsistent practices of the leadership, see p. 43.

14. The bibliographical data have been conveniently assembled by N. Roth, "Deal Gently With the Young Man: Love of Boys in Medieval Hebrew Poetry of Spain," *Speculum* 57 (1982): 20–51.

15. See the literature cited by J. Schirmann, "The Ephebe in Medieval Hebrew Poetry," *Sefarad* 15 (1955): 57, n. 4, and add N. Aloni, "*Haṣevi vehagamal beshirat sefarad*," *Oṣar yehude sefarad* 4 (1961): 16–43.

16. Text in Ḥ. Schirmann, *Shirim ḥadashim min hageniza* (Jerusalem: Publications of the Israel Academy of Sciences and Humanities, 1965), p. 158. Where I have Absalom, the text reads Adonijah. The latter was the brother of the former, who was vain of his great head of hair, and who, according to good medieval authority cited by Schirmann, was the one intended by Ibn Mar Saul. Metrical considerations that compelled the original poet to substitute Adonijah compelled me to restore Absalom.

17. P. Dronke, *The Medieval Lyric* (New York: Harper & Row, 1968), pp. 86–108 cites analogies from many medieval European cultures.

18. References in Schirmann, "The Ephebe," p. 59, n. 13. For similar sexual

ambiguousness in medieval European literature, see J. M. Ferrante, *Woman As Image in Medieval Literature From the Twelfth Century to Dante* (New York: Columbia University Press, 1975), p. 4.

19. Uncourtly love does not seem to be a theme of Arabic poetry either; see Pérès, *La poésie andalouse*, p. 425.

20. Schirmann, *Hashira haʿivrit*, 1:155. For my free translation of the story, see D. Stern and M. Mirsky, *Rabbinic Imagination* (Philadelphia: Jewish Publication Society, in press). I have dealt with the theme of the two kinds of love in my paper, "Fawns of the Palace and Fawns of the Field," to appear in *Prooftexts* 6 (1986).

21. See Denomy, *The Heresy of Courtly Love*, pp. 20–32; on the neo-Platonic roots of this conception, see G. E. Von Grunebaum, "Avicenna's *Risala fi 'l-ʿIšq* and Courtly Love," *Journal of Near Eastern Studies* 11 (1952): 233–238. Because Schirmann interpreted Hebrew love poetry using a strict criterion of sexual versus spiritual he was led to some false emphasis in his article "*L'amour spirituel dans la poésie hebraïque du moyen age*," *Les Lettres Romanes* 15 (1961): 315–325.

22. *William Shakespeare: The Sonnets*, introd. by W. H. Auden, ed. W. Burts (New York: Signet, 1965), p. xxix.

Poem 11

Source:
    Schirmann, *Hashira haʿivrit*, 1:370.
Translation:
    Carmi, *Penguin Book*, p. 324.

1. See Introduction, n. 11.
2. Stern, *Hispano-Arabic Strophic Poetry*, p. 14.
3. Similar expressions in Moses Ibn Ezra's poetry are thoroughly indexed by Pagis in Brody, *Moshe Ibn Ezra*, 3:341–342, s.v. "*semikhuyot leteʾur.*"
4. The Arabic original of the book is lost. A Hebrew epitome of the thirteenth century refers to it as "*Meqor ḥayyim.*"
5. See Abraham Ibn Ezra's commentary on Gen. 2:8.
6. The play was actually a sort of bilingual pun in the Arabic-speaking environment, since the root ʿ*ashaq*, which in Hebrew means "to oppress," means "to love" in Arabic.
7. The phrase originated in Deut. 21:11. For an example of its use as a technical term, see Babylonian Talmud, Qiddushin 21b.
8. *Nevel*, used to mean both "bottle" and "lute," as in poem 3; *sis* (rejoice); ʿ*asis* (wine); *sis* (swallow).
9. Gen. 19:5–11 (Lot and the men of Sodom); Judg. 19:22–27 (the Ephramite's concubine in Gibeah); Songs 5:2–6 (the lover's nocturnal visit).
10. Exod. 29; Lev. 8.

Poem 12

Source:
    Schirmann, *Hashira haʿivrit*, 1:367–368.
Translations:
    Roth, "Deal Gently With the Young Man," pp. 45–46.
    Carmi, *Penguin Book*, pp. 325–326.

NOTES

1. Hamori, *On the Art of Medieval Arabic Literature*, p. 38.
2. Maimonides, *Mishne torah, Shevuot* 12:11; Commentary on the Mishna, *Shevuot* 4:1, ed. Kafaḥ, p. 263.
3. Ezek. 48:35.
4. Songs 8:2: "I would lead thee, and bring thee into my mother's house." Targum: "King Messiah led you and brought you to the Temple." Perhaps the poet also had in mind Songs 3:4, where the phrase also occurs.
5. The rabbinic source material was collected by A. Aptowitzer, "The Heavenly Temple in the Agada," (Hebrew) *Tarbiz* 2 (1930–1931): 137–153; 257–287.
6. This exposition is opposed to that of Brody in *Moshe Ibn Ezra*, 3:7, and Schirmann, *Hashira haʿivrit*, 1:368, who seem to think that love grounded in philosophy must be asexual.

Poem 13

Source:
Schirmann, *Hashira haʿivrit*, 1:369.
1. A. Mirsky, "Mashmaʿut heharuz beshirat sefarad," *Leshonenu* 33 (1959): 150–195; Monroe, *Hispano-Arabic Poetry*, p. 20.
2. See the introduction to Chapter I.
3. I.e., the consonants *nhshty* representing an original *lhshty* or *rhshty*, meaning "to speak," as in liturgical poetry.

Poem 14

Source:
Schirmann, *Hashira haʿivrit*, 1:153.
Translations:
Weinberger, *Jewish Prince*, pp. 122–123.
S. M. Stern, "ʿĀšiqayn Iʿtanaqā," *Al-Andalus* 28 (1963): 155–170.
1. Joseph Ibn Sahl. The *kharja* appears also in an Arabic poem. For full references, see J. T. Monroe and D. Swialto, "Ninety-Three Arabic Ḫarǧas in Hebrew Muwaššaḥs: Their Hispano-Romance Prosody and Thematic Features," *Journal of the American Oriental Society* 97 (1977): 145 and n. 10.
2. Another reading, "*ya shaqqain*," would mean, "Ah, two parts which have both embraced . . ."; this also stresses the dual number.
3. Job 1:15.
4. Ibn Ḥazm, *The Ring of the Dove*, p. 23; emphasis mine.

Poem 15

Source:
Schirmann, *Hashira haʿivrit*, 1:214.
1. II Sam. 13.
2. For the story of the concubine in Gibeah, see Judg. 19.
3. For full references, see Wagner, *Abu Nuwas*, p. 291, n. 2. See also the translation by A. Wormhoudt, *The Diwan of Abu Nuwas al-Ḥasan ibn Hani al-Ḥakami* (Oskaloosa, Iowa: William Penn College, 1974), p. 154.
4. Ibn Dawud al-Isfahani, *Kitab al-zahra*, ed. A. R. Nykl in collaboration with I. Tuqan (Chicago: University of Chicago Press, 1932), pp. 29–36.

NOTES

Poem 16

Source:

Schirmann, *Hashira ha'ivrit*, 1 : 68.

Translation:

Carmi, *Penguin Book*, p. 283.

1. See the introduction to this chapter, p. 88.

2. This is not, of course, the literal meaning, but the verse is obscure. See Maimonides, *Mishne Torah, Ishut* 13 : 11.

3. Schirmann, *Hashira ha'ivrit*, 1 : 575. The translation here seems to be by N. Ausubel in his *Treasury of Jewish Humor* (Garden City, N.Y.: Doubleday & Company, Inc., 1952), p. 448.

4. Moses Ibn Ezra, *Kitab al-muhadara*, p. 58.

Poem 17

Source:

Schirmann, *Hashira ha'ivrit*, 1 : 438.

Translation:

B. Martin, in *A History of Jewish Literature* ed. I. Zinberg (Hoboken, N.J.: Ktav, 1972), 1 : 88.

1. The method upon which much of this analysis is based is developed for Arabic in my *Form and Structure*. On enjambment, see pp. 11–15. For a strikingly similar placement of an adjective of color, see pp. 90–91. The same principles apply to Golden Age Hebrew verse.

2. Pérès, *La poésie andalouse*, p. 402; Ibn Ḥazm, *The Ring of the Dove*, pp. 61 and 64.

Poem 18

Source:

Schirmann, *Hashira ha'ivrit*, 1 : 446.

Translation:

Martin in Zinberg, *A History of Jewish Literature*, 1 : 88.

Poem 19

Source:

Brody, *Diwan des Abu al-Ḥasan*, 2 : 16.

Poem 20

Source:

Schirmann, *Hashira ha'ivrit*, 1 : 439.

Translations:

Goldstein, *Hebrew Poems*, p. 120.

Carmi, *Penguin Book*, p. 343.

Martin in Zinberg, *History of Jewish Literature*, 1 : 88.

1. The translation of the verse is by D. L. Smith, *The Poems of Mu'tamid King of Seville* (London: John Murray, 1915), pp. 16–17.

NOTES

Poem 21

Source:

Schirmann, *Hashira ha'ivrit,* 1:155.

Translation:

Weinberger, *Jewish Prince,* p. 122.

Roth, "Deal Gently With the Young Man," p. 36.

Poem 22

Source:

Schirmann, *Hashira ha'ivrit,* 1:215.

Discussion:

Adi Ṣemaḥ, *Keshoresh 'eṣ* (Jerusalem: Akhshav, 1962), pp. 101–110.

1. For this point and several others I am indebted to the discussion by Ṣemaḥ.

2. This type of rhythmic analysis is based on my work on Arabic poetry. See my *Form and Structure,* pp. 125–132.

3 DEATH

Introduction

1. Pagis, *Shirat haḥol vetorat hashir,* pp. 215–216; I. Levin, *'Al Mot* (Ramat Gan: Tel Aviv University, 1973), pp. 164–206.

2. Wagner, *Abu Nuwas,* p. 129, n. 6.

3. For the accusation and a refutation, see G. Vajda, *"Les zindiqs en pays d'Islam au début de la période abbaside,"* Rivista degli Studi Orientali 17 (1938):215–220.

4. F. Gabrieli, "Religious Poetry in Early Islam," in *Arabic Poetry: Theory and Development,* ed. G. E. von Grunebaum (Wiesbaden: Otto Harrassowitz, 1973), p. 17.

5. Abu ʾl-'Atahiya, *Diwan,* ed. L. Cheikho (Beirut: Jesuit Press, 1887), p. 23. Verse translation in R. A. Nicholson, *A Literary History of the Arabs* (Cambridge, England: Cambridge University Press, 1956), p. 299.

6. In Hebrew, *Ben mishle* and *Ben qohelet,* literally, *"Son of Proverbs"* and *"Son of Ecclesiastes."*

7. See Chapter I, n. 15.

8. See pp. 22–23.

9. Text in P. Birnbaum, *High Holiday Prayer Book* (New York: Hebrew Publishing Company, 1951), p. 791; also in Carmi, *Penguin Book,* pp. 207–208.

10. *Avot* 3.1.

11. An interesting poem that does dwell on the macabre is found in Carmi, *Penguin Book,* pp. 248–250.

12. Schirmann, *Hashira ha'ivrit,* 1:588. A less elaborate poem on the same theme is included in this anthology as poem 29.

13. See especially poem 16.

14. J. Huizinga, *The Waning of the Middle Ages* (Garden City, N.Y.: Doubleday & Company, Inc., 1954), p. 141.

Poem 23

Source:
 Schirmann, *Hashira ha'ivrit*, 1 : 372.
Translations:
 Goldstein, *Hebrew Poems*, p. 78.
 Carmi, *Penguin Book*, pp. 323–324.
 Solis-Cohen and Brody, *Selected Poems*, pp. 40–41.
 1. Songs 1 : 12; translated by M. H. Pope in *Song of Songs: The Anchor Bible* (Garden City, N.Y.: Doubleday & Company, Inc., 1977), p. 292.
 2. See my discussion of the use of parallelism in closure in *Form and Structure*, p. 125.
 3. Job 31 : 33.
 4. Hos. 8 : 4.
 5. Found already in Ps. 102 : 10.
 6. Gen. 3 : 13.

Poem 24

Source:
 Schirmann, *Hashira ha'ivrit*, 1 : 136.
Translations:
 Goldstein, *Hebrew Poems*, p. 43.
 Weinberger, *Jewish Prince*, pp. 129–130.
 Carmi, *Penguin Book*, p. 295.
 Bargebuhr, *The Alhambra*, pp. 354–355.
 Hamori, *On the Art of Medieval Arabic Literature*, pp. 92–94.
Discussion:
 Bargebuhr, *ibid.*
 Hamori, *On the Art of Medieval Arabic Literature*, pp. 94–98.
 1. Hamori, *ibid.*, p. 96.

Poem 25

Source:
 Schirmann, *Hashira ha'ivrit*, 1 : 202.
Translations:
 Carmi, *Penguin Book*, p. 306.
 Goldstein, *Hebrew Poems*, p. 65.
Discussion:
 Semah, *Keshoresh 'eṣ*, pp. 15–21.
 Levin, *'Al Mot*, pp. 113–114.
 1. The text of the long poem may be found in Schirmann, *Hashira ha'ivrit*, 1 : 196–201; discussed in Levin, *ibid.*, 9–19.

Poem 26

Source:
 Schirmann, *Hashira ha'ivrit*, 1 : 132.
Translations:
 Goldstein, *Hebrew Poems*, p. 44.

NOTES
191

Weinberger, *Jewish Prince,* pp. 130–131.
Carmi, *Penguin Book,* p. 285.
1. See poem 24.

Poem 27

Source:
   Schirmann, *Hashira ha'ivrit,* 1:133.
Translation:
   Weinberger, *Jewish Prince,* pp. 96–97.
Note: In the translation I have taken the liberty of moving verse 13 of the original, placing it after verse 9. There is no manuscript authority for the change.
   1. Mirsky, "*Mashma'ut heharuz,*" p. 190.
   2. Eccles. 3:19–21.
   3. Eccles. 12:13.
   4. This is, in fact, Abraham Ibn Ezra's interpretation of Eccles. 12:13.

Poem 28

Source:
   Schirmann, *Hashira ha'ivrit,* 1:403.
Translation:
   Carmi, *Penguin Book,* p. 329.

Poem 29

Source:
   Schirmann, *Hashira ha'ivrit,* 1:131–132.
Translation:
   Weinberger, *Jewish Prince,* p. 127.
   1. Qohelet Rabba 1:2.
   2. Schirmann, *Hashira ha'ivrit,* 1:588–590. "Sinews" translates a felicitous emendation in the Hebrew text, suggested by Schirmann.

Poem 30

Source:
   Schirmann, *Hashira ha'ivrit,* 1:136.
Translation:
   Weinberger, *Jewish Prince,* pp. 128–129.
Discussion:
   Levin, *'Al Mot,* pp. 84–85.
   1. The word translated "exempted" literally means "protected," but my translation has some justification in R. P. A. Dozy, *Supplément aux dictionnaires arabes* (Leiden: E. J. Brill, 1881), 1:329, s.v. "*hmw.*"

Poem 31

Source:
   Schirmann, *Hashira ha'ivrit,* 1:230–231.
   1. The Talmud, in Eruvin 13b, considers whether it would not have been better

for man never to have been created. See J. J. Petuchowski, *Theology and Poetry: Studies in the Medieval Piyyut* (London: Routledge & Kegan Paul, 1977), pp. 98–110.

2. A courtier of King David's mentioned in II Sam. 23:8. The name, later made famous by al-Ḥarizi as the title of a book (see Introduction to Chapter I, n. 9) was understood to be derived from the Hebrew word meaning "sage."

3. Schirmann, *Hashira ha'ivrit*, 1:208.

For Further Reading

In exploring an unfamiliar literature, it is helpful to have some knowledge of the historical circumstances surrounding it. Fortunately, two very readable books exist in English that not only provide the beginner with the historical facts of the Golden Age but also depict the style and tone of the culture. The history of the Muslims in Spain, from the conquest to about 1100 (i.e., approximately fifty years before the end of the period covered in the present volume) has been elegantly told by a Dutch scholar, Reinhart P. A. Dozy, whose book was originally published in French in 1861. The book has since been revised and in some respects superseded by more recent histories written in other languages; but the beautiful English translation by Francis Griffin Stokes, entitled *Spanish Islam: A History of the Moslems in Spain* (London, 1913; repr. 1972), is a classic and a delight to read. The history of the Jews in Spain to 1085 is the subject of a work by Eliyahu Ashtor, originally written in Hebrew but now available in a slightly abridged form in English under the title *The Jews of Moslem Spain,* translated by Aaron Klein and Jenny Machlowitz Klein (3 vols.; Philadelphia, 1973–1984).

Readers who wish to penetrate more deeply into the lives and mentality of the courtier-rabbis in whose circle secular Hebrew poetry developed should read a book that has been referred to several times in this work, Gerson D. Cohen's *Sefer ha-Qabbalah: The Book of Tradition* (Philadelphia, 1967). Cohen's work is a study of a twelfth-century historical treatise. His introduction to the treatise gives a clear picture of its historical and cultural background. Following the Hebrew text and its English translation, Cohen explicates the view held by the medieval author and his peers about Jewish history and the role of the Andalusian courtier-rabbis therein.

A brief presentation of the history of Islamic Spain that devotes systematic attention to literature and the arts is *A History of Islamic Spain* by W. Montgomery Watt (Edinburgh, 1965). The reader of the present volume will probably wish to learn more about the Arabic poetry of Muslim Spain. The fullest picture in English of this rich literature is given by A. R. Nykl in *Hispano-Arabic Poetry and its Relation with the Old Provençal Troubadours* (Baltimore, 1946; repr. 1976), which, though reprinted, is not widely available. The virtue of this book is its anecdotal approach to the poets and the copious selections of their poetry contained therein. There is also an anthology of Arabic poems from Spain with English translations and a fine introduction by James T. Monroe, entitled *Hispano-Arabic Poetry: A Student Anthology* (Berkeley, 1974).

On the Jewish literature that developed against the background of Arabic letters, there is a good comprehensive essay by Abraham S. Halkin, "Judeo-Arabic Literature" in *Great Ages and Ideas of the Jewish People*, edited by Leo W. Schwartz (New York, 1956). A more extensive treatment of Judeo-Arabic culture, with continual reference to its literary aspects, is S. D. Goitein's popular *Jews and Arabs: Their Contacts Through the Ages* (3rd ed.; New York, 1974).

Few of the prose writings of the Golden Age have been translated into English, but these books, mostly written in Arabic, must be read for the intellectual background to the poetry that they offer. A pietist's reaction against the worldly outlook of the courtiers, Baḥya Ibn Paquda's *Book of Direction to the Duties of the Heart* provides a fascinating corrective to the picture given in the present work. This book has been translated by Menaḥem Mansoor et al. (London, 1973). A minor treatise by Ibn Gabirol, *The Improvement of the Moral Qualities*, was translated by Stephen S. Wise (New York, 1902). Ibn Gabirol's complete philosophical work, *The Fountain of Life*, is available in Latin and Hebrew translations. The Hebrew translation, entitled, *Meqor Ḥayyim*, is by Jacob Blubstein (Jerusalem, 1925–1926). Only a selection of the work can be read in the English translation by Harvey E. Wedeck (New York, 1962). But Judah Halevi's *Kuzari*, which can be read in several different Hebrew versions, is available in an English translation entitled *Kitab al Khazari*, translated by Hartwig Hirschfeld (London, 1905; repr. 1927 and 1964). There is a good abridged edition with a commentary by Isaak Heinemann, entitled *Kuzari: The Book of Proof and Argument* (Oxford, 1947); and selections from this work may be read in *Three Jewish Philosophers*, edited by Alexander Altmann (New York, 1960).

The only extensive systematic account in English of the Hebrew poetry of Golden Age Spain is contained in Israel Zinberg's *A History of Jewish Literature, Vol. I: The Arabic Spanish Period*, translated and edited by Bernard Martin (Hoboken, N.J., 1972). This book was originally published in Yiddish in 1929; though outdated and not authoritative, it provides a good introduction. A concise survey of Golden Age Hebrew poetry within the context of medieval Hebrew poetry in general is Shalom Spiegel's essay "On Medieval Hebrew Poetry" in *The Jews: Their History, Culture and Religion* (3rd ed.; 1960), 1 : 854−892; also reprinted in *The Jewish Expression*, edited by Judah Goldin (New York, 1970), pp. 174−216.

The four great poets of the Golden Age can be sampled in individual volumes already frequently referred to in this work. They are: Leon J. Weinberger, *Jewish Prince in Moslem Spain: Selected Poems of Samuel Ibn Nagrela* (University, Alabama, 1973); Israel Zangwill and Israel Davidson, *Selected Religious Poems of Solomon Ibn Gabirol* (Philadelphia, 1924; repr. 1974); Solomon Solis-Cohen and Heinrich Brody, *Selected Poems of Moses Ibn Ezra* (Philadelphia, 1945); and Nina Salaman and Henrich Brody, *Selected Poems of Jehudah Halevi* (Philadelphia, 1924; repr. 1974). Each of these volumes has an introduction summarizing what was known of the author's life at the time of writing. Most of these could be revised today. The works of several important poets, including Abraham Ibn Ezra, are not yet available in individual volumes. There is, however, a sketchy anthology by David Goldstein, *Hebrew Poets from Spain* (London, 1965; reprinted as *The Jewish Poets in Spain, 900−1250*, 1983). The reader is already familiar with T. Carmi's thorough *Penguin Book of Hebrew Verse* (New York, 1981) which contains selections from many Golden Age poets not included in the present volume, and which also displays the Golden Age in the context of the entire history of Hebrew poetry. One major poem by Ibn Gabirol has become a whole book in English. It is *The Kingly Crown*, translated with an introduction and notes by Bernard Lewis (London, 1961).

Readers who know or who are studying Hebrew are fortunate to have at their disposal the wonderful anthology by Ḥayyim Schirmann, *Hashira ha'ivrit bisefarad uveprovans* (2 vols.; Jerusalem and Tel Aviv, 1954−1956; 2nd ed.: 4 vols., 1960−1961). This masterful book gives extensive selections of the works of the four great poets and representative selections from every poet of any importance at all. There is a biographical and critical introduction to each poet; the poems are provided with explanatory notes; the book concludes with an extensive bibliography, an introduction to medieval Hebrew versification, and a glossary of technical terms. It is a beautifully designed book, with pictures of illuminated manuscripts, architectural monuments, and topographic features that help in understanding the poetry.

Another book that Hebrew readers should be aware of is Schirmann's *Shirim ḥadashim min hageniza* (Jerusalem, 1965). More than 150 pages of this monumental work are devoted to recently discovered poems by Golden Age poets. The introductions to the individual poets update their bibliographies. Though intended for the use of specialists, this book contains much material of interest to the general student of Hebrew literature. Several monographs are available in Hebrew that provide necessary literary background and analysis for the study of this field. David Yellin's *Torat hashira hasefaradit* (Jerusalem, 1940; repr. 1972) deals with the rhetorical conventions of the poetry and their relationship with those of Arabic poetry. Dan Pagis' *Ḥidush umasoret beshirat haḥol* (Jerusalem, 1976) studies the various uses of this rhetoric in the different genres of the poetry. Pagis has also written an important book on the relationship between poetic theory and practice in the writings of Moses Ibn Ezra, entitled *Shirat haḥol vetorat hashir lemoshe ibn ezra uvene doro* (Jerusalem, 1970). This book derives its information about poetic theory largely from Moses Ibn Ezra's own treatise on poetics, originally written in Arabic. This book has been published twice, in editions cited earlier, p. 182 n. 27. Books on medieval Hebrew poetry continue to appear in Israel, thanks in part to the growing interest of some Israeli poets in the history of their craft. This essay does not purport to be a complete listing of every important book in the field, but only a starting point for the interested student.

Index

INDEX
201